# The Divine Purchase

# The Divine Purchase

Douglas Vickers

WIPF & STOCK · Eugene, Oregon

THE DIVINE PURCHASE

Copyright © 2015 Douglas Vickers. All rights reserved. Except for brief quotations in critical publications or reviews, no part of this book may be reproduced in any manner without prior written permission from the publisher. Write: Permissions. Wipf and Stock Publishers, 199 W. 8th Ave., Suite 3, Eugene, OR 97401.

Wipf & Stock
An Imprint of Wipf and Stock Publishers
199 W. 8th Ave., Suite 3
Eugene, OR 97401

www.wipfandstock.com

ISBN 13: 978-1-4982-2618-9

Manufactured in the U.S.A.                                    08/18/2015

Scripture quotations are from the King James Version.

With gratitude to
*Ann Hopkins*
without whose literary skill
and collaboration over many years
much less would have been accomplished

# Contents

*Preface* | ix

1 The Human Condition | 1
2 In the World | 13
3 Covenantal Structure | 24
4 The Divine Personhood of Christ | 38
5 The Divine Purchase | 49
6 Partakers of Redemption | 60
7 The Cosmic Significance of Christ | 70
8 The Christian's Benefit in Christ | 81
9 Adoption | 93
10 The Imperative of Faith | 103
11 The Knowledge of God | 115
12 The Necessity and Canonicity of Scripture | 128

*Bibliography* | 141

# Preface

THE TITLE I HAVE chosen, *The Divine Purchase*, is motivated by the statement of Paul the apostle to the elders of the church at Ephesus as he returned from his third missionary journey: "God purchased the church with his own blood." My intention in this book is to bring into relationship a number of biblical doctrines that bear on the accomplishment and application of redemption as that was due, in its most intense meaning, to Christ's substitutionary offering of himself for the sins of those whom God the Father gave to him to redeem. I look directly at that important piacular work of Christ in the topic chapter 5. The importance of what is at issue rests in the fact that as Christ himself said, he came to give his life a ransom for his people. The ransom price that was paid calls for our meditation in the highest degree.

In the early chapters of the book I have endeavored to indicate briefly the necessity of redemption. That emanates from the determinate divine council that established the covenantal structure of God's dealings with the human race, notably with those whom he chose to redeem. That covenantal structure brings into immediate prominence the personhood of Christ, the only propitiator for sin and the only mediator between God and man. On the other side of the necessity of redemption, the human condition is explored as that is exhibited by the implications and the bequest of Adam's fall.

The later chapters address the on-going results of the purchase that the Son of God effected, in both the larger and cosmic significance of the work of Christ and the application of it to the Christian believer. The concluding chapters recapitulate briefly some principal themes and expand on the knowledge of God and the necessity and canonicity of Scripture. Those chapters address a number of highly significant questions that follow from the basic presuppositions that underlie the work. Those include the presuppositions that *God is*

## Preface

and that *God has spoken*. The final chapter aims to justify the presupposition that *God has spoken* by examining the relevance of the Scripture that has been extensively adduced in the preceding chapters.

No man thinks well who thinks alone. In the intellectual disciplines we are each other's keepers. My deepest thanks are accordingly due to those who have assisted me in the preparation of this book. I acknowledge a heavy debt of gratitude to the Rev. Dr. Robert E. Davis, who has for many years encouraged my transition to writing in doctrinal theology following my retirement from a professorship in a non-theological academic discipline. Informed readers will recognize that, in the apologetic aspects of the book, I am influenced by the path-breaking work in that area of the late Cornelius Van Til, and I record my admiration for, and gratitude to him. In a long list of books and professional papers I have benefited enormously from the editorial assistance of Ann Hopkins, and I record my deepest thanks to her for her unfailing skill and cheerfulness in bringing my work to publication. I dedicate this book to her with affection and gratitude.

For the blemishes and infelicities that remain in the book I am entirely responsible.

CHAPTER 1

# The Human Condition

ON THE LEVEL OF human understanding, and on the grasp of the meaning of the individual self, a number of questions engage the reflective mind. They do not arise with necessarily high or equal degrees of articulation in all instances and in all conditions and socio-cultural environments. But the realities of human personhood are such that the equanimity of everyday is inevitably disturbed, and the issues involved press for awareness and clamor for recognition. First, what is the meaning of individual personhood, its being and its life-journey, and its significance in the normal course of affairs? Second, in the light of personhood, what is to be said of one's participation in the complex relations on which the journey proceeds, and his contribution to the forms and structures of those relations? Third, what is to be contemplated as the end, the terminus, to which answers to those questions point and which casts its light on the journey itself? For surely, the conclusion does not call for expanded argument that to travel well cannot in itself exhaust the reason for being. There is conceivably an end, a reason for, and a purpose in the travel that conjures its own significant meaning.

Our questions have enjoyed a long currency in the history of thought, in instances too numerous to rehearse in detail, though the answers they have attracted have been various. They have recurred in the frequent aphorism, "Know thyself" (γνῶθι σεαυτόν, *gnōthi seauton*), of classical Greek philosophy. The poet, Alexander Pope, took up the theme in the eighteenth century and concluded his *Essay on Man* with the lines: "Know then thyself, presume not God to scan; / The proper study of mankind is Man."[1] In the following century Samuel Taylor Coleridge began his brief poem,

---

1. Pope, *Essay on Man*, in Abrams, *Norton Anthology*, 770.

*Self-Knowledge*, with the same Greek adage, and in his concluding line he observed: "Ignore thyself, and strive to know thy God."[2]

But most forcibly, John Calvin has pondered the questions in the opening lines of his *Institutes* and has placed them in their true and elevated significance: "Nearly all the wisdom we possess, that is to say, true and sound wisdom, consists of two parts: the knowledge of God and of ourselves. But, while joined by many bonds, which one precedes and brings forth the other is not easy to discern. In the first place, no one can look upon himself without immediately turning his thoughts to the contemplation of God . . . Again, it is certain that man never achieves a clear knowledge of himself unless he has first looked upon God's face, and then descends from contemplating him to scrutinize himself."[3]

Following Calvin, let us set aside for a moment our initial questions and reflect on what is now to be contemplated as a question of prior import, that of the knowledge of God. Here, then, further questions arise. First, why, and on what grounds, is knowledge of God possible? And second, given that such knowledge is possible, what is to be said of the manner of its acquisition by man, and what may be understood as the potential content of it? In the history of thought again, much ink has been spilt in discussions of questions such as these. Involved on a broader level is the large and philosophic question of what is referred to as epistemology, the questions of the origin, process, and validity of knowledge. We shall make contact with such issues in the chapters that follow. It will be necessary to ask, for example, how it is possible to claim that God exists, if, in fact, our system of thought is grounded in, and takes its legitimacy from God's existence. That very question has been the hunting ground of thinkers both within and outside of the Christian church. Some have claimed that logical proofs of the existence of God can be established. Indeed, certain Christian thinkers have argued that the essential province of Christian theological apologetics lies on precisely that level. The apologetic task, it is said, is first to establish the existence of God and then, in the light of the result achieved, to consider the substance of theological doctrine and dogmatics that follows. What is involved in such claims is the assumption that, as it may be stated, apologetics is prior to theology. It is not difficult to suspect that an incipient rationalism, or argument based on the presupposition of the competence of human reason, lies at the foundation of such systems of thought.

---

2. Coleridge, *Self-Knowledge*, in *Complete Works*, 487.
3. Calvin, *Institutes*, 35, 37.

## The Human Condition

But it may be more legitimately and substantially claimed, not that apologetics precedes theology, but that the reverse is true. Theology is prior to apologetics. That is so, not only because of the finitude of human reasoning and its possible scope in the areas we are now investigating, but because also of the necessary structure of human thought and investigation itself. All reasoning is necessarily grounded in some form or other of presuppositional foundations. And in the complex of the questions we are now addressing, that of the knowledge of God as prior to and determining the legitimacy of the knowledge of self, our basic apologetic presupposition is twofold: first, *God is*; and second, *God has spoken*. But if we say that, we are proposing that any more extensive argument that engages us will be of a unique form as to its elements, sequences, and conclusions. If, then, Christian thought proceeds in its uniquely established fashion because it is grounded in the fact that *God has spoken*, it will acquire its flavor, not from the assumption that argument proceeds from man to God, but from the fact that it proceeds from God to man. Another way of saying the same thing is that because God has spoken into existence all things external to the Godhead, all things are his property, and all things acquire their meaning only as they are understood as occupying their place and function in God's eternal purpose. That of course implies that man himself is the creature of God. He did not emerge from a primeval slime, or come into being as a metamorphosis of a pre-existing, pre-human entity. Man is the creature, the covenantal and responsible creature, of the Creator-God.

Why, then, is it possible to know God? The knowledge of God is possible because God has made a gracious revelation of himself. God has declared his being and has manifested his glory in various ways. Man himself, by reason that he was created as the image of God, is revelatory of God. The very heavens declare the glory of God (Ps 19:1). God has revealed himself and his purpose in the history of the world and of the human race, most notably in the history of his people in Old Testament times. He has graciously inscripturated his revelation. And he has "in these last days spoken unto us by his Son, whom he hath appointed heir of all things, by whom also he made the worlds" (Heb 1:2). It follows from the very nature and extent of God's revelation that all men know that *God is* and that he has spoken. There are no atheists. That is to say, there are no people who do not know that God exists. In that sense we say that there are no psychological atheists. There are, of course, those who can be said to be practical atheists, people who live as though God did not exist. But in the very structure of their thought and claims they are living a lie. "Because that which may be known of God is manifest in them; for God hath showed it unto them. For the invisible things of him from the creation of the world are clearly seen, being understood by the things that are made, even his eternal power and Godhead; so that they are without excuse" (Rom 1:19-20). The fault is not in any lack of clarity in the revelation that God has made. The revelation is thoroughly clear. The fault is in the fact that man in his state of sin and voluntary estrangement from God has put blinkers on his eyes so that he cannot see. The problem is that when the awareness of God rises unbeckoned to the level of consciousness men naturally suppress it, push it down below the level of cognition. They press down the truth in unrighteousness (Rom 1:18).

What, then, has God revealed? Or what is the possible scope and extent of the knowledge that man in his finitude may possess? The answers to those questions will be explored more fully in the following chapters. But for the present, two things can be said by way of preliminaries. First, as we go on to observe that man as created is the image of God, we shall take note of the fact that man is the analogue of God, both as to his being and his knowledge. On the level of our immediate concern with man's knowledge capacities and abilities, we shall say that what man knows of God is the analogue of what God knows in himself. In other words, man can know God truly, but he cannot know God comprehensively. The prophet Isaiah has stated: "My thoughts are not your thoughts, neither are your ways my ways, saith the LORD. For as the heavens are higher than the earth, so are my ways higher than your ways, and my thoughts than your thoughts" (Isa 55:8-9). It is open to question, of course, whether the immediate reference of God's statement at that point has to do with the thought of God in the matter of the provision of salvation, or, as we have suggested in the present context, with the relation between God and man as to the structure and capacities of thought in general. Both levels of interpretation are clearly relevant.[4]

Second, God has given to man a natural revelation in, as we have seen, the universe of reality that he has spoken into existence. That natural revelation is sufficient to make man not only truly aware of God but responsible to him, and to place man under judgment by God for his sinful delinquency in life and behavior. But that natural revelation does not convey to man the way of reconciliation with God. It does not convey the gospel of salvation. God has contained that gospel in the Scriptures. But to understand what

---

4. See the discussion of Isa 55:8-9 in Young, *Isaiah*, 3:382-83.

## The Human Condition

is involved in God's inscripturated revelation the following should be held in mind. First, God has made to man, in all the ways we have envisaged, a partial revelation of himself. Second, the Scriptures, in turn, contain a partial record of that partial revelation. It is as John has observed at the end of his gospel: "There are also many other things which Jesus did, the which, if they should be written every one, I suppose that even the world itself could not contain the books that should be written" (John 21:25). Third, by reason of what we have already observed as the nature and capacities of human understanding, we have only a partial grasp and understanding of that Scriptural revelation. Our abilities to grasp and understand the content of the inscripturated revelation is deficient by reason of our inherited sinful state and the effects on the mind, the noetic effects, of Adam's fall. So that at best, man has only a partial understanding of the partial inscripturation of the partial revelation of himself and his purposes that God has made. But that partial understanding that rests on our finitude is graciously sufficient to make known to sinful man the way of reconciliation with God, redemption from the guilt of sin, and eternal life and security in the presence of God.

In the light of what has now been said we return to our initial questions. What is man, and what explains the human condition? At this initial stage we make some minimal summary statements, the relevance of which will be expanded at more length as we proceed. First, man as created is the image of God. "And God said, let us make man in our image . . . in the image of God created he him, male and female" (Gen 1:26–27). We do not say that God at first created man and then in some sense imposed his image on him. We do not say, therefore, that man *bears* the image of God. We are saying that man *is* the image of God. That has been put more formally as follows:

> "Man, created soul and body, male and female, is the *image of God* in that he is *an immortal, rational, spiritual, moral,* and *speaking* person, capable of *reflective self-awareness* and *purposive action,* characterized in his created condition by *knowledge* and by *constitutive holiness and righteousness,* and endowed with the capacity for the reception of divine revelation, social relations and communication, and communion with God his Creator."[5]

To say that man *is* the image of God is to make a very different claim from the statement that man *bears* the image of God. First, he is immortal. The Scriptures state that God "breathed into his nostrils the breath of life, and man became a living soul" (Gen 2:7). We say that man *is* body and soul,

---

5. Vickers, *The Cross,* 10.

and in reference to his personhood we refer to man in his bodily aspect and man in his soulish aspect. When we say that man is soul, we are saying that he is *spiritual*. The nature of the soul that man is, is such that he is the derivative analogue of God. He has derivative immortality. Because he is what he is, he will necessarily live forever. The reality, however, is that now, as a result of the entrance of sin, that immortality will be lived out forever in a state of eternal separation from God or, in the case of those whom God has redeemed, in the presence of God in Christ forever.

Second, man is rational. He possesses the faculty of thought and imagination and reflective self-awareness. Man thinks, because God thinks. He understands because God has implanted within him the faculty of soul that is capable of investigating the meaning and explanation of things. He is endowed with the faculty of seeing things in their ordered or their logical relations. That is why it is to be said that the laws of logic are the same for the Christian and the non-Christian. The difference between them has to do with the use that they make of the laws. The laws of right thinking are not something of human invention. Logic is a divine endowment. But a sharpness of intellect that is biased in the unregenerate person by the effects of his state in sin, whose logic is therefore capable of running on a biased and irrelevant track, will not reach valid conclusions regarding one's relation to God.

Third, man as the image of God was created a speaking person in order that he can understand the meaning of God's speech to him, that he can speak back to God the meaning that he discovers in reality, and that he might enjoy communion with God.

Fourth, man is a moral being because God is moral. God has revealed himself as a moral being in that all his actions, thoughts, and ordinations are consistent with the eternal holiness in which he exists. Man, therefore, is moral in that he is capable of judgments between right and wrong behavior and action. He sustains a responsibility for decisions and choices of action, and he is accountable to God for the manner in which he discharges his moral responsibility in relation to the law of God.

What has been said involves the fact that man is characterized by derivative personhood because absolute personhood exists in God. In his status as the image of God, man knows truly only as and when he knows God truly, and as he thinks God's thoughts after him. In the state in which he came from the hands of his creator, man was constituted in knowledge, holiness, and righteousness. We are saying, that is, that man's original holiness

## The Human Condition

was an aspect of his initially constituted state. He was constitutionally and intrinsically holy by reason that he was the image of God. We do not hold, as do some theologies, that our first parent's holiness was a characteristic that was added on to his initial state after he came to being and self-consciousness. Adam's initial holiness was not a *donum superadditum,* a gift-added-on. But as the Westminster Shorter Catechism states, man did not continue "in the estate in which he was created." He fell from that estate by sinning against God.[6] Our objective at this point is to say that while man at the fall was deprived of the knowledge, holiness, and righteousness that he had at first possessed, he continued to be the responsible and accountable image of God. Man, that is, continues to be a rational, immortal, spiritual, moral, and speaking person.

When we say that man was created as the image of God, we are saying that man was like God in every respect in which, in finite personhood, he can be like his infinite Creator. Man, that is, is the analogue of God, both as to his being and his knowledge. As created, with full faculties of human soul, intellect, emotion and will, man naturally knew God, he naturally loved God and the law of God communicated to him, and with a naturalness of will be obeyed God. Moreover, it is clear that in his pristine state the faculty of mind or intellect was the prince of the faculties of the soul. That is established by the fact that God articulately communicated with Adam, that in his prelapsarian speech to him he conveyed the content and meaning of his law and our first parent's mandates and responsibilities in relation to that law. Adam understood God's speech to him and the substance of what God had communicated, and he accordingly responded to God. We have it in Genesis 3:8 that "God walked with Adam in the garden in the cool of the day."

But Adam fell. The image of God was marred and, as we shall see more fully, the faculties of soul were depraved and disabled as to their knowledge of God. The guilt of Adam's sin was imputed to all that were to come from him by natural generation.[7] At his creation, and as constitutive of God's purpose in creation, Adam was established as the federal head or representative of all of his natural posterity. When Adam sinned, they were all then guilty in the sight of God by reason of their participation in Adam. As to the human condition, then, all people are naturally at sinful enmity against God (Rom 8:7). It is not the case that all men are sinners

---

6. Westminster Shorter Catechism, Questions 13–19.

7. See ibid., Question 16.

because they commit sin. The reverse is true. All men commit sin because they come into the world as sinners, with a fallen, sinful nature. All men were constituted sinners at Adam's fall. That is the terrible reality of the human condition. "By one man sin entered into the world, and death by sin; and so death passed upon all men, for that all have sinned" (Rom 5:12). "By one man's [Adam's] disobedience many were made sinners" (Rom 5:19). "In Adam all die" (1 Cor 15:22). "All have sinned, and come short of the glory of God" (Rom 3:23). And as a result, our Lord said to certain of the Jews on one occasion, "Ye are of your father the devil, and the lusts of your father ye will do" (John 8:44). "The carnal mind is enmity against God; for it is not subject to the law of God, neither indeed can be" (Rom 8:7). Such is the sorry state to which the fall brought mankind.

Two things are to be said of our first parent's state of soul in his initially created state. First, there existed, as we have seen, a natural harmony among the faculties. With the mind Adam naturally knew God, with the heart he naturally loved God, and with the will he naturally obeyed God. And second, the mind was the prince of the faculties of the soul. But as a result of the fall, first, the pristine harmony of the faculties was shattered; and second, the mind was dislodged from its status of hegemony, or leadership, in the soul, and the soul was now ruled by the lusts and the passions. It is important to anticipate on those grounds that when we consider the movement of the soul to salvation in Christ, the work of regeneration that the Holy Spirit accomplishes in the soul is preeminent at precisely that point. Regeneration reestablishes the hegemony of the mind, and the first appeal of the gospel, accordingly, is an appeal to the mind. We shall return to those important issues.

In speaking of our first parent as he stood in his initial state, we have referred to the capacities of the faculties of soul with which he was endowed. In doing so we are employing the language of faculty psychology. In the history of theological doctrine, referring at this stage to the doctrine of biblical anthropology or the doctrine of man, differences of view have been held as to the legitimate use of the psychological categories that have been employed. For consider what we refer to respectively as the mind or the intellectual faculty, the emotional capacities or the affective faculty, and the will or the volitional faculty. Now an extensive dispute has arisen as to the proper understanding of the potential interrelation between those faculties. What may be denoted an improper faculty psychology is the claim that the respective faculties are capable of independent action. Indeed, a historic system of theology known as Arminianism, which continues to have wide currency at the present time, holds that the will is capable of determining its own action. It is to the credit of the early American philosopher-theologian, Jonathan Edwards, that his treatise on *The Freedom of the Will* was written precisely to controvert that claim, and to explain that in human conduct all the faculties of soul are active in concurrent and interactive determination. In short, the will is not free to determine its own action but necessarily acts as instructed by, and as determined by, the intellectual and emotional faculties.[8] It is important to note again by way of anticipation that when we consider the movement of the sinner to repentance and saving faith in Christ, it will be observed that in those actions the whole person, in the mutual engagement of all of his faculties of soul, is active.

Let us reflect a little more on the original mandates, offices, and responsibilities that God gave to Adam. He was constituted, we can say, in the offices of prophet, priest, and king. The distinguishing responsibility of the prophetic office is that of explanation. We see that as we observe that the office of the Old Testament prophets, for example, was to explain to God's people his requirements of them. Adam's office as prophet required him to investigate and explain the reality environment in which he had come to self-awareness and with which God had blessed him. His office as priest was to dedicate that discovery and explanation back to the glory of God. His office as king was to rule over all of created reality as God's vicegerent, to "Be fruitful, and multiply, and replenish the earth, and subdue it; and have dominion over [it]" (Gen 1:28).

The effects of Adam's fall, and the implications for all men since, is that they are thereby disabled from fulfilling those creation mandates and thereby fulfilling God's requirements of them. The fact that all people in their natural state and condition are, as a result, unable to please God in those initially mandated respects is of overriding importance. The implication of it needs to be seen, at least briefly at this stage, in terms of the covenant obligations that God imposed on our first parents.

Adam was, we have said, God's covenant creature. Man is a covenant being. In the history of theological doctrine, particularly in the Reformed tradition, God's relation with Adam has been construed in covenantal terms. The covenant of creation, frequently referred to also as the covenant of works, was unilaterally established by God who, in terms of it, made certain promises to Adam conditional on his performance of specified

---

8. Edwards, *Freedom of the Will*, 73, 86.

conditions or obligations. Not all Reformed theologians prefer to make use of the nomenclature, covenant of works.[9] But the initial divine-human relation, it can be said, is properly construed in those terms.[10] The stated terms of Adam's probation are clear. "Of every tree of the garden thou mayest freely eat. But of the tree of the knowledge of good and evil, thou shalt not eat of it: for in the day that thou eatest thereof thou shalt surely die" (Gen 2:16–17). Differences of view have been held as to the implicit promise contained in that probationary directive. But it is widely and properly understood that if Adam had sustained his probation and had obeyed his maker and not eaten of the forbidden fruit, he would have been confirmed in righteous moral state and rewarded with eternal life.

It is clearly stated in the scriptural data that the first Adam was a type of the second Adam, Jesus Christ (Rom 5:14). And it is clear that the second Adam (see 1 Corinthians 15:45, 47) was rewarded for his obedience to the requirements of the covenant of grace. "When he had by himself purged our sins [he] sat down on the right hand of the Majesty on high; being made so much better than the angels, as he hath by inheritance obtained a more excellent name than they" (Heb 1:3–4). And "God also hath highly exalted him, and given him a name which is above every name; that at the name of Jesus every knee should bow" (Phil 2:9–10). Further, "In the dispensation of the fullness of times [God will] gather together in one all things in Christ, both which are in heaven, and which are on the earth; even in him" (Eph 1:10). On the grounds that the first Adam was a type of the second Adam, and that the second Adam was in the ways we have indicated rewarded for *his* obedience, the conclusion is warranted that Adam, if he had sustained his probation and had not sinned, would have been rewarded for *his* obedience. He would have been raised to eternal life. The works to which Adam was obligated, in addition to his refraining from eating of the forbidden tree, were, firstly, his discharging to the glory of God what we noted previously as his offices of prophet, priest, and king; and secondly, his obedience to the laws of morality that God communicated to him.

But for purposes of the conclusion we have in view regarding the present human condition, a highly significant implication of the covenant of

---

9. See, for example, the distinguished twentieth-century Reformed theologian, John Murray's *Covenant of Grace* and the same author's "Covenant Theology" in Murray, *Collected Writings*, 4:216–40, and "The Adamic Administration" in *Collected Writings*, 2:47–59.

10. A positive discussion of the covenant of works, together with a response to dissents from it, is included in Vickers, *Divine Redemption*, 26–73.

## The Human Condition

works remains. It should be borne in mind that the terms of the covenant of works constitute what are properly referred to as creation ordinances. By creation ordinances we refer to those communications, directives, and ordinances that were divinely given to Adam in his pristine state before he fell into sin. Because they were thereby given to man as man in his standing before God, by the very fact that they are *creation* ordinances they are obligatory on all people everywhere and at all times. It follows that the obligations of the covenant of works were not abolished when Adam fell, but that they remain incumbent on all people at the present time. They remain the criteria of judgment in the eternal state that is to come. In short, those who, at the Day of Judgment, go to eternal perdition will have received that assignment on the ground that they have not in this life fulfilled the requirements of the covenant of works.[11]

The realities of the human condition are such that, by reason of the entailment of sin in which they are bound, none of Adam's natural posterity is able either to fulfill the offices to which he was first appointed, or to keep and honor the obligations of the covenant of works which, as has been seen, continue to rest upon them. Is there no ground, therefore, on which reconciliation with God can ensue? It is precisely at that point that the glory of God's gospel of saving grace enters. As Hodge has stated it, "This covenant having been broken by Adam, not one of his natural descendants is ever able to fulfil its conditions, [but] Christ having fulfilled all of its conditions in behalf of all his own people, salvation is offered now on the condition of faith."[12]

When we come to a fuller statement of the terms of the gospel we shall see that Christ was the substitute under the law of God for all those whom the Father had given to him to redeem (John 17:6). "Why did Jesus Christ come into the world?" it may be asked. The answer resides on many levels. But from what has now been said, it follows that Christ came to do for us, his people, what we were obligated to do under the covenant of works but could not do for ourselves because we were disabled by our bondage to sin. Because Christ was our substitute in those profound respects, because he not only kept the law of God perfectly on our behalf but died to pay the penalty for our sin, because his forensic righteousness was imputed to us and our guilt was imputed to him, two results follow in the accounting of

---

11. See the fuller discussion in Vickers, *Divine Redemption*, 26–73, and Hodge, *Outlines of Theology*, 314.

12. Hodge, idem.

heaven. God now looks on us as though we had ourselves kept his law; and he looks on us as though we had ourselves paid the penalty for having broken the law. So complete is the respect in which God the Father has placed to our account all that Christ has done for us and on our behalf.

At the beginning of this chapter we raised the second question that engages the mind. What is to be contemplated as the end, the terminus, of life's journey? The outlines of the answer that will engage us further are now clear. The end of all things is either eternal life in the presence of our Savior on the one hand, or eternal perdition on the other. The bearing on those alternatives, and the reasons for the conclusions that are relevant, will engage us in the following chapters.

CHAPTER 2

# In the World

THE NECESSARY PRESUPPOSITION OF Christian thought, we observed in the preceding chapter, is that *God is* and that *he has spoken*. In making that statement, what is being spoken about is the presupposition of *Christian* thought. For the non-Christian, who has not been the beneficiary of the renewing work of the Holy Spirit in the soul and who stands, therefore, in implacable enmity against God, the natural presupposition of thought is completely different. In his case, determined as it is by the false assumption of autonomy against God, the foundation of his thought turns on the assumed competence of unaided human reason. His basic postulates are the subject of his autonomous, independent choice from whatever has passed through his mind or is available for selection from the intellectual fashions of the world around him. But for the Christian, subject as his intellectual life is to the word of God as he has revealed himself in the Scriptures, his presuppositions are themselves supplied to him by the word of God. His every thought, therefore, is captive to Christ in whom God has made his final revelation. The Christian has learned, as the apostle argued, to bring "into captivity every thought to the obedience of Christ" (2 Cor 10:5). The non-Christian autonomously and sovereignly chooses his presuppositions or plucks them from the air. The Christian receives his presuppositions as supplied to him by the word of God.

The character and status of the non-Christian derives from his participation in the fruits of Adam's fall. The Westminster Shorter Catechism clarifies that again by saying that "The covenant being made with Adam, not only for himself, but for his posterity, all mankind, descending from him by ordinary generation, sinned in him, and fell with him, in his first transgression."[1] As a result, "The fall brought mankind into an estate of sin and misery."[2] Consider our father Adam's position. In his initial state, we have said, the mind was the prince of the faculties of the soul. But Satan attacked our first parent at precisely his highest point. And at that point Adam's sin was born. He was confronted by the mandate of God, which he knew clearly in his prelapsarian state. He was not to eat of the forbidden tree. At the same time, he was confronted by the claims of the tempter. Now the question arose in his mind as to whom, and which of the respective statements submitted to him, he should obey. Was it to be God, whom he clearly knew as his Creator and gracious communicator, or the devil? In the upshot, Adam decided that he would believe neither of the claims before him simply on the grounds of the identity of the presenter. Rather, Adam would make up his own mind and decide for himself. At that very point the false and damning assumption of human autonomy had entered. Fallen man has assumed his autonomous competence ever since. The truth and validity of what he knows is adjudicated against the criteria proposed by assumedly competent unaided human reason. At Adam's fall, human intellection was shifted decisively to the track of autonomy, and it has continued to explain the essence of the sinful state ever since.

As a result, the intellectual life of the natural man has been captive to the same damning and determining assumption of autonomy. The Scriptures are eloquent on the point. "The god of this world hath blinded the minds of them which believe not, lest the light of the glorious gospel of Christ, who is the image of God, should shine unto them" (2 Cor 4:4). That is the terrible status of the man who is a sinner at his very birth into the world. The reality is that we come into this world with a fallen nature. But it would not be correct to say that we are sinners *because* we come into the world with a fallen nature. Something more profound is at issue. We come into the world with a fallen nature because, by virtue of our union with Adam as our federal head, we were constituted sinners at Adam's fall. And whatever is to be said from that point on, the implication is not that we are sinners because we commit sin, but that we sin, and that we sin naturally, because we are sinners. That state and condition resulted from the imputation to us of the guilt of Adam's first sin. Man in his natural state, therefore, is the blinded dupe of the devil. He sins, and he sins naturally, because he is captive to Satan and sin. Our Lord stated that on a memorable occasion

1. Westminster Shorter Catechism, Question 16.
2. Ibid., Question 17.

## In the World

in the course of a disputation with the Jews. "When a strong man armed keepeth his palace, his goods are in peace" (Luke 11:21). Satan, the "strong man armed," keeps his "goods," those who are captive to him in the peaceful slumber and somnolence of sin, and they are unable even to think any thought of righteousness. Such is their sorry state. Or listen to the apostle Paul as he explained the matter to the Corinthian church: "The natural man receiveth not the things of the Spirit of God; for they are foolishness unto him; neither can he know them, because they are spiritually discerned" (1 Cor 2:14). It is not only that the unregenerate person does not grasp and understand the truth of the gospel of God's grace. The unbeliever does not understand because he cannot understand. He is blind. He has deliberately put blinkers on his eyes to prevent his seeing and understanding. In doing that he has, with his father Adam, turned his back totally on the obligations that are placed upon him by virtue of God's initial covenantal statements. In short, sin is the repudiation of covenantal obligations.

If mankind, in that way, is enslaved to sin in his intellectual faculty, what is to be said, in turn, of his faculties of emotion and will? At Adam's fall, the faculties of soul were not destroyed. Man remains the image of God in that he is still a rational, immortal, spiritual, moral, and speaking person. But the faculties were disabled from performing their pristine functions, and they were now bent and biased away from seeing and knowing and obeying and loving God as he had at first covenantally revealed himself. Man still thinks and feels and acts. But in all those respects he is no longer able to place himself under the gracious hands of God, to think God's thoughts after him, and to fulfill the covenantal obligations originally placed upon him. The early indictment of God has remained and its import intensified: "God saw that the wickedness of man was great in the earth and that every imagination of the thoughts of his heart was only evil continually" (Gen 6:5).

We may examine further, at least briefly, two aspects of what is involved in the statements that have just been made. First, what are we to understand as the "world" from whose domain, as we shall see, the believer in Christ has freedom, considering the "world" in all of its intellectual, moral, and ethical dimensions? And second, we shall consider at a later point what, as a result, is to be the Christians believer's relation to the world as its claims continue to press upon him. Let us take the first point first.

Foremost importance is to be attached at this point to the respects in which certain developments in intellectual history have led to the condition at the present time in which the doctrinal theology of the church, and thereby the security of the ordinary life of the Christian, is under heavy attack. It is not necessary (though the exercise would be highly relevant and profitable) to digress to take notice of certain theological heresies that have provided intellectual background to the present state of things. The early Arian and Sabellian heresies are capable of recurring recrudescence;[3] Pelagian digressions raise their head, and various forms of human autonomy squeeze their way into the church.[4] At the present time, various alien philosophies exert their influence on the church and its doctrines. There is, of course, a genuine biblical philosophy, as there is a biblical philosophy of history and of human conduct. There is a genuine biblical philosophy of being (metaphysics), knowledge (epistemology), and behavior (ethics). But the warning of the apostle is nevertheless urgent: "Beware lest any man spoil you [take you captive] through philosophy and vain deceit, after the tradition of men . . . and not after Christ" (Col 2:8). But that is the point at which the church continues to be troubled. There is a true "philosophy after Christ." But the conclusion appears unavoidable that the view of Christ has become too low in modern times because the view of man has become too high. Let us look at some minimal details.

The assumption of human autonomy that we have referred to has been historically prominent. It entered philosophic thought decisively at the hands of Descartes in the seventeenth century. After confining himself in seclusion for a day, as history has it, he decided that he would base his belief-system only on what he had concluded were "clear and distinct ideas." The most significant clear and distinct idea that he came to realize was that of his own existence and intellection. His famous "I think, therefore I am," *cogito ergo sum*, immediately elevated the human mind to the level of autonomous deliberation regarding the locus of truth. That highly significant

---

3. Arianism, which was refuted by the church at the Council of Nicea in the year 325AD, argued that Jesus Christ was not eternally God, the Second Person of the Godhead, but that he was a created entity. Sabellianism, a heresy current at the same time, claimed that what the theology of the church referred to as the Second and Third Persons of the Godhead, God the Son and God the Holy Spirit, were not distinguishable eternal Persons, autotheotic and fully God in their own right, but that the three "persons" were only emanations of the one God. Sabellianism has come back to currency in forms of Unitarianism.

4. Pelagius, who flourished in the fourth century and whose claims were refuted in a controversy with Augustine, argued that the faculties and capacities of the human soul were not affected by Adam's fall and that, as a result, while man was obligated to obey God he was perfectly able to do so if he so wished and chose.

step in intellectual history having been taken, it is important for our present discussion to take note of the contribution of Immanuel Kant at the end of the so-called eighteenth-century Enlightenment. Kant had made a uniquely important step forward, as he saw it, in his epistemological theory, the theory of the origin, processes, and validity of knowledge. The essence can be stated briefly, the grasp of which is necessary to understanding the state of the church's theology at the present time.

Two principal elements of Kantian thought call for notice in our present context. First, Kant argued that reality was to be understood as divided into two so-called realms: the phenomenal realm, the realm of things, or the perception of things, that could be seen and handled; and the noumenal realm, in which entities, genuine realities, might be thought possibly to exist. Knowledge, then, was confined or limited to what was observable in the phenomenal realm; or more particularly, it was confined to an individual's perception of what was existent in that realm. For it was not the "things in themselves," the *ding an sich*, but the phenomenal representations of them, that were knowable. We shall see in a moment how, in fact, such possible knowledge came to exist. But what might or might not exist in the noumenal realm was not knowable. For theology, Kant's critical step at that point was that he consigned God to the noumenal realm. God, Kant therefore said, might or might not exist. It was not possible to know. At the same time as Kant concluded that it could not be known or proved that God existed, it was equally true, he charitably said, that it was not possible to prove that he did not exist.

Before we move to the second important element of Kant's thought, the element that has been referred to in the history of thought as Kant's "Copernican revolution" in the theory of knowledge, let me indicate briefly Kant's stated position on the possible existence of God. The upshot was that Kant argued that the existence of God could not be demonstrated as an element of "pure reason," but that it could conceivably be a usable, and even a necessary assumption of "practical reason." In his *Critique of Practical Reason* he argued that "It is morally necessary to assume the existence of God [but] this moral necessity is *subjective*, that is, it is a want, and not *objective*."[5] That conclusion follows from Kant's earlier argument in his *Critique of Pure Reason*: "These remarks will have made it evident that the ideal of the Supreme Being, far from being an enouncement of the existence of a being in itself necessary, is nothing more than a *regulative principle* of reason . . . it

---

5. Kant, *Critique of Practical Reason*, 109.

exists merely in my own mind, as the formal condition of thought, but not as a material and hypostatic condition of existence."[6] Kant's influence on doctrinal theology has continued to the present time in its liberal expressions, and the critical element has been that of the unknowability of God.

But that very development has meant and implied that the ground of reason and knowledge is not to be found in the revelation that God has given, but in the assumption of the competence of unaided human reason. That, in a sentence, is the continuation, in many parts of contemporary theology, of what we have already identified as the pervasive assumption of human intellectual autonomy. It could be argued, if larger space were available at this time, that a corresponding assumption of the competence of unaided human reason informs certain evangelical apologetic arguments.

The elevation of the virus of assumed autonomy in Kantian thought is clear in the second element we anticipated in Kant's epistemological philosophy. What the individual perceives in the phenomenal realm is transformed into knowledge, Kant claimed, by the application to those perceptions of certain so-called "categories," or "forms of understanding" resident in the mind. A rehearsal of those "categories" is not necessary, except to say that their use in the determination of knowledge means in effect that the individual does not see or know reality as it is, but that reality is, for him, how it is constructed by his own mind. Every man determines his own reality. One historian of thought has put that by saying that for Kant "The world is not an objective fact independent of us, to be defended and criticized as such. It is the product of the laws of our own understanding."[7] That is the assumption of autonomy come to its fullest expression.

The Christian believer, we shall go on to see, has been delivered from the world and from the damning postulate of autonomy. Paul states to the Galatian church that "Christ gave himself for our sins, that he might deliver us from this present evil world, according to the will of God and our Father" (Gal 1:4). For the Christian, contrary to the dictates of every form of non-Christian argument, does know that God exists and has spoken in the revelation of himself and his purposes that he has made. Christianity is a "we know" religion. The contents of what the Christian knows can, of course, be stated at length and will be referred to more fully. But it is all, in a sense, summed up in our Lord's statement in his high priestly prayer:

---

6. Kant, *Critique of Pure Reason*, 306–307.

7. Rogers, *History*, 378.

"This is life eternal, that they might know thee the only true God, and Jesus Christ whom thou hast sent" (John 17:3).

But what, it is still necessary to ask, is "the world," from the domination and realm of which the Christian has liberty? First, the world, it follows from all we have said to this point, is fallen human nature that is fashioning human society in accordance with its own tendencies, the presuppositions and prescriptions of the "carnal mind" that is "enmity against God . . . not subject to the law of God, neither indeed can be" (Rom 8:7). The world is the deliberate rejection of God. It, and life within it, is anthropocentric, man-centered, in the ultimate degree. It is the realm in which the intellectual autonomy against God has come to expression in moral and ethical autonomy. In his letter to the Ephesians, Paul referred to the state of the Gentiles before the doors of the kingdom of God were thrown wide open to them (see Gal 3:14). They were (i) without Christ, (ii) aliens from the commonwealth of Israel, (iii) strangers from the covenants of promise, (iv) having no hope, and (v) without God. And then, in order to summarize and drive home the meaning of all that as it applied to the Gentiles and the hopelessness of it, he says that they were (vi) "in the world" (Eph 2:12). That is the strength of the indictment against all those who are outside of Christ. They are "in the world," and the world is the realm in which God is deliberately shut out.

Further, "the world" from which the Christian is to be distinct conjures a cast of mind that is not only in fact but, with a conscious deliberateness, opposed to God. It will have nothing to do with God. God is excluded from all its thought-systems. As to the occupants of "the world," "There is no fear of God before their eyes" (Rom 3:18). Those who are still "in the world" live with the display of the reality of God and the display of his goodness before their eyes. Every man knows that God is, the apostle to the Gentiles has told us in the first chapter of his letter to the Romans, and the consciousness of God, the *sensus deitatis*, is inherent in the soul of every man by reason of his creation as the image of God. But the reality is that whenever that awareness of God rises unbidden to the level of consciousness it is suppressed again (Rom 1:18) and man chooses to live outside of God. If any cognizance of God should be admitted, those "in the world" instinctively react by setting out to "prove" the existence of God on the grounds, as we have seen, of the presupposition of the competence of unaided human reason. The declarative statements of the Scriptures that *God is* and that *he has spoken*, are deliberately rejected. "God" for the world that still lives in darkness is a god made in the image of human imagination.

To expand briefly on what has already been said we may remark further on the state of man "in the world." We have taken note indirectly of the assumption of *metaphysical autonomy* (metaphysics, or ontology, has to do with the nature and essence of being). That amounts to the assertion that man has not come from the hands of a sovereign Creator-God. Our first parent, it is then agued, was not the unique creation of God who had said, "Let us make man in our image" (Gen 1:26). He may be thought to have evolved from lower forms of life; or he may have emerged as a representative of a certain tribe, or community of man-like entities. But in whatever form such notions may be held, man, in the characteristic thought forms of the world, is what he is, morally and culturally, because he claims autonomy against God. All of that amounts to the fact that man has denied his creaturehood. To the extent that the thought forms of the "world" are adopted, man has no explanation of himself. Contrary to the fact that God has spoken all things into existence and that all things happen according to his providence and eternal purpose, a widespread assumption of contemporary postmodernism is that all that happens happens by chance. But if that is claimed to be so, then man himself is a chance phenomenon, the reality of individual responsibility and accountability is destroyed, and there is no longer any grounding for personal ethics. Such is the meaning of "the world" from which the Christian and his fellowship with the Father is distinct in being, knowledge, and behavior.

Further, a critically important implication that warrants observation is the projection from metaphysical autonomy to the epistemological autonomy that we observed as leading from Kant. We should now see that the common assumption of man in the world is that, for him, the real criteria of truth and validity in knowledge are not those that God has set forth in his law and revelation (see Gen 3:8, where God "walked with Adam in the garden in the cool of the day" and conversed with him). Rather, the false assumption is made that man can establish his own criteria of truth by observing moral and cultural norms as they exist in society around him and by bringing his own thought into confluence with them. Or he may derive his knowledge criteria simply from his own cogitation and imagination as to how he should live.

But what we have observed as *metaphysical* and *epistemological autonomy* point clearly to the fact that, on the level of behavior and conduct, the

## In the World

natural person claims for himself also *ethical autonomy*. That is, the criteria of right conduct and behavior are again not those found in the moral law that God has delivered, but, it is supposed, are to be found within man himself or culled from contemporary social and cultural norms. Or once again, as the criteria of belief and of truth are for the natural man excogitated from within man himself or are found in the social nexus that surrounds him, it follows that for the natural, unregenerate person, his true status is what it is because, denying God, his life, knowledge, and conduct are determined by false assertions of metaphysical, epistemological, and ethical autonomy.

Such are the characteristics of life "in the world," from which the Christian is to separate himself in being, knowledge, and behavior. He is to "love not the world, neither the things that are in the world" (1 John 2:15). He is to resist the enticements of the world that would drag him down to a level below his true identity. The apostle John continues and draws a clear dichotomy between the Christian and the man of the world. "If anyone loves the world, the love of the Father is not in him." That is to say, such a person has no love for God within himself, nor, of course, can he, apart from the renewing work of the Holy Spirit within him. The love that the Father bestows on his children "is not in him," he has no part in it, and he is altogether outside the range and scope of the Father's paternal love.

The apostle John advances a further reason for not conforming, in thought, belief, or action, to the world. "The world passeth away, and the lust thereof; but he that doeth the will of God abideth for ever" (1 John 2:17). If one is foolishly, sadly, shortsightedly committed to the love of the world and the things in it rather than to the love of God, it can only be said of him that he will never find peace, comfort, security, fulfillment, or satisfaction, and that he has been deluded into forgetting that his end is coming, the world is passing away. The day of glory on the one hand and judgment on the other will dawn.

History laughs at the sinner. He imagines that the world provides him with the stability he seeks. But that is his highest and saddest fallacy. The world is passing away. History moves on the linear trajectory of divine intent. The day is coming, the great eschatological terminus, when "in the dispensation of the fullness of times [God will] gather together in one all things in Christ, both which are in heaven and which are on earth" (Eph 1:10). Then those who, by the grace of God, have learned the joys of the privilege of fellowship with God in this life will rise to the "inheritance

. . . predestinated according to the purpose of him who worketh all things according to the counsel of his own will" (Eph 1:11).

What, then, are we to say of the human condition and the life of man in the world? Contemporary belief regarding the nature and condition of man distances itself from the biblical doctrine that we have adduced. It is captive to the thought forms of evolutionary anthropology. Man came from the mud, it is imagined, even though his destiny lies with the stars. The story of man as it is seen from that perspective is one of a long ascent. It is the story, it is said, of a magnificent journey. As the nineteenth century matured and gave place to the twentieth, the concept of the perfectibility of man was aided and abetted by wider fashions in social and scientific thought that saw horizons optimistically broadening. But the events of what began as the century of the common man have sobered opinions. The wars of the century, the economic depressions, and the clear collapse of culture and social cohesion that has accelerated to the present time have tarnished the earlier optimism. Something is wrong at the very heart of man and his culture. His life is twisted and decaying away from intelligible meaning. His morals have lost what was once their secure moorings, and his social complexes display a seediness and exhaustion.

The real story of man, however, is not one of a long ascent. It is a story of a beginning in a condition of unimaginable bliss, followed by a catastrophic fall. The story is one of a descent towards the retribution for dereliction from the demands of the covenant that God established with man at his creation. It is true that God has intervened, first at the very beginning in establishing a covenant of grace by which man would be rescued from the entailment of his sin, and secondly, by the administration of his common grace. God's immanent intervention by his common grace has been responsible for the restraint that has inhibited the fuller development of the darkness and the depravity of human sin, and it is responsible also for the positive development of scientific progress and human culture.

But the entrance of sin implied that at the fall man suffered both a *deprivation* and a *depravation*. By the entrance of sin, man was completely undone. His state of original holiness and righteousness was lost, connoting his deprivation, and his whole nature was corrupted, reflecting his depravation. Now he was depraved in all of the faculties of soul. Now he had lost communion with God and he stood, instead, under the wrath and the curse of God. Now he was liable to all the miseries of this life that were entailed upon the entrance of sin, and he stood subject to the prospect of eternal perdition for his sin. There could be no alleviation and no escape from the penalty for sin unless God should intervene and provide a way of redemption.

But God intervened. It is the glory of the gospel of God's grace that he provided a way of redemption and reconciliation with himself by sending his Son into the world to provide redemption from sin. He came, the apostle John said, "that he might destroy the works of the devil" (1 John 3:8). And the writer of the epistle to the Hebrews states that he came in order that "He might destroy him that had the power of death, that is, the devil" (Heb 2:14). We turn immediately in the following chapter to reflect on the covenantal structure of God's intentions, purpose, and actions that have been graciously directed to those ends.

CHAPTER 3

# Covenantal Structure

IF COGENCY OR TRUTH attaches to what has been said to this point, the question arises, "How can man be right with God?" That was the cry of Job long ago, "How should man be just with God?" (Job 9:1). The answer, in short, is that God "sent his Son to be the propitiation for our sins" (1 John 4:10). "Jesus Christ came into the world to save sinners" (1 Tim 1:15). The terms of the gospel of saving grace are spread liberally across the pages of Scriptures. The data of Scripture are eloquent on the divine salvific intention. They disclose clearly the terms of God's covenantal design by means of which the objective of redemption was consummated. We shall summarize briefly in what follows the essence of what is involved.

Biblical theology is covenant theology. We have already said that sin is to be understood in an ultimate sense as the repudiation of covenantal obligations. We have seen that our first parent's sin implied precisely such a repudiation. The state and condition of all his natural posterity turns on the facts that, first, the guilt of Adam's first sin was placed to their account by imputation; second, by immediate imputation at the point at which Adam fell, those descendants were constituted sinners; third, they all come into this life with a fallen nature that precludes their knowledge of the grace of God and fellowship with him; and fourth, as they are thereby enslaved to Satan and sin, their very actions are inevitably actions of sin.

We may put the point differently. At the fall, man lost his free will. When it is asked whether our first parents "continued in the estate wherein they were created," the Catechism answers: "Our first parents, *being left to the freedom of their own will*, fell from the estate wherein they were created, by sinning against God."[1] Free will, as to man's ability to know God for who

---

1. Westminster Shorter Catechism, Question 13, italics added.

he is as the God of grace and to obey his commandments, has been surrendered by man's capitulation to slavery and bondage to sin. The case does not need extensive argument. The apostle Paul clarified it once and for all in his letter to the Romans: "To whom ye yield yourselves servants [Greek δούλους, *doulous*, slaves] to obey, his servants [slaves] ye are to whom ye obey; whether of sin unto death, or of obedience unto righteousness" (Rom 6:16). Notwithstanding the surrender of free will, human free agency, of course, continues. But free agency involves simply the freedom to act according to one's nature. That applies to all of God's sentient creation. A horse is free to be a horse, to do horse things and nothing else. A cow is free to be a cow. The Scriptures have made the point. Consider, for example, a sow, as in 2 Peter 2:22. It is possible to take the sow and wash it from its filth and natural habits. But as soon as one's back is turned from the dressed-up sow, the outcome is all too obvious. "The sow that was washed is returned to her own wallowing in the mire." The poor creature was nothing but a sow. And all it could do was things consistent with being a sow. So it is with the sinner. The sinner is free to act according to his nature. But because his nature is essentially sinful, the sinner is free only to act and behave sinfully.

To say the same thing differently, man is free to choose what it is that his dominating desire presents to him as his decided preference. The eighteenth-century American philosopher-theologian, Jonathan Edwards, clarified that when he argued that an individual will necessarily choose according to what appears to him as his "greatest apparent good." "Every act of the will is some way connected with the understanding, and is as the greatest apparent good is."[2] Or as Edwards states it again: "It is impossible for the will to choose contrary to its own remaining and present preponderating inclination."[3] The reality is that that final preponderating inclination in man is subject to, and determined by, the "bias" that resides in the soul because of his captivity to sin.[4]

What, then, are the covenantal arrangements that God has made in order to rescue the human situation? An extensive theological literature exists to answer the question. But the essence of what is involved can be brought under the headings of the covenants that God has established: the covenant of redemption, the covenant of works, and the covenant of grace. Some theologians have put the matter by speaking of a bi-covenantal

2. Edwards, *Freedom of the Will*, 86.
3. Ibid., 73.
4. Idem.

theology. By that is meant holding to the covenant of works on the one hand, and collapsing the covenants of redemption and grace into one covenantal construction. Some theologians, on the other hand, prefer not to speak of a covenant of works, also referred to as the covenant of creation, made by God with Adam, and they prefer to take what has been referred to as a monocovenantal position. The details can be summarized briefly in what follows.[5]

The covenant of redemption refers to the voluntary commitment and undertaking of the Persons of the Godhead as the outcome of their deliberations in the council of the Godhead before the foundation of the world. The moment we make such a defining statement, of course, we pause to realize that here the mystery of the divine trinity in being and action is engaged. For God is the necessary divine being who, in triune personhood, exists in timeless eternity and who created time as a mode of our finite existence. We are then speaking anthropomorphically (in language with which we have been endowed in our finitude and humanness) when we use "in time" language to make any reference to the intracommunication of the divine Persons of the trinity who exist outside of time. But as to the covenant that followed from the divine council, it is possible and necessary to observe in the Scriptures that each of the three Persons of the Godhead, in their distinguishable personhoods, undertook specifically designed redemptive offices. The grasp and clarification of those respective offices call for address for our present purposes.

First, the fact of the divine redemptive council is clear from scriptural declarations. All that occurs in history eventuates because of, and in accordance with, the dictates of the will of God. There is no more ultimate explanation of anything or of any entity or event than the will of God. The reasons for the determinations of the will of God are, of course, beyond our grasp or apprehension. We said in an earlier context that the mind of God and the deliberations of his will are incomprehensible to us. It was said that our knowledge is the analogue of God's knowledge that he possesses in himself. It is available to man to know God truly, but not to know him comprehensively. "The secret things belong unto the LORD our God; but

---

5. Herman Witsius, a distinguished seventeenth-century Dutch Reformed theologian, has provided a definitive treatment of this subject in his *Economy of the Covenants*. Other discussions are contained in numerous systematic theologies. Some paragraphs in this chapter, at points relating to the forms of God's covenantal administrations, have been reproduced from chapter 4, "The Covenant-Making God," in Vickers, *Texture of Truth*.

## Covenantal Structure

those things which are revealed belong unto us and to our children" (Deut 29:29). But that the deliberations of the triune Godhead lie beyond and determine the process of redemption is clear.

The apostle Paul crystallized the issue when he said to the Ephesians that the inheritance of the people of God has been "predestinated according to the purpose of him who worketh all things after [or according to] the counsel of his own will" (Eph 1:11). Paul states in Acts 20:27 that he had declared "all the counsel of God." Psalm 33:11 says: "The counsel of the Lord standeth forever." Again, in his sermon on the day of Pentecost, Peter stated clearly to the Jews that Christ was "delivered by the determinate counsel and foreknowledge of God" (Acts 2:23). Soon thereafter, when the church met in prayer on the occasion of the arrest and subsequent release of Peter and John following their healing of the lame man, their prayer included the recognition that those who crucified our Lord did "whatsoever thy [God's] hand and thy counsel determined before to be done" (Acts 4:28). Similarly Paul, in the magnificent first paragraph of his letter to the Ephesians said that we were "predestinated . . . unto adoption of children" because God has "chosen us in him before the foundation of the world" (Eph 1:4). Finally, Peter, in a statement that throws its light on what we shall refer to as the redemptive offices of the Persons of the Godhead, makes the same claim by referring to us as "elect according to the foreknowledge of God the Father, through sanctification of the Spirit, unto obedience and sprinkling of the blood of Jesus Christ" (1 Pet 1:2). Other scriptural statements to the same effect abound, such as Romans 8:29–30: "Whom he [God] did foreknow, he also did predestinate to be conformed to the image of his Son . . . Moreover whom he did predestinate, them he also called; and whom he called, them he also justified; and whom he justified, them he also glorified."

The redemptive office of the Father was that of choosing (as the texts cited above reveal) a certain, definite, and unalterable number of people who, according to his will, would be redeemed from sin in order to share his eternal glory with him. Those persons whom the Father elected and chose to eternal salvation he gave to his Son to redeem. That is clearly declared in our Lord's high priestly prayer as we have it recorded in the seventeenth chapter of John's gospel: "Thine they were, and thou gavest them me" (John 17:6). Further, his prayer continued at that time, "Holy Father, keep through thine own name those whom thou hast given me" (John 17:11), and "I pray not for the world, but for them which thou hast given me; for they are thine" (John 17:9).

## The Divine Purchase

Differences of view have been held as to the identity, in a specific sense, of those whom God the Father elected. Some theologians have held that those who were elected (we refer to them as the subjects of the decree to elect) were, in fact, beings whom God intended to create and that they were created with the end of election in view. If such a position were held, the subjects of election would be understood to have been creatable, but not created, people. At the timeless point of the decree of God (here we confront again the difficulty of speaking of a point in a timeless divine context) the subjects of election were identifiable as such before the fall of Adam that made redemption necessary had occurred. That form of doctrine is therefore referred to as *supra*lapsarianism (the prefix "supra" referencing "before the fall"). On the other hand, many theologians have taken full cognizance of the reasons for the need of redemption, and in doing so have held that the subjects of the decree to redeem were, in fact, fallen people. Their position is therefore *infra*lapsarian ("infra" referencing "after the fall"). Clearly, mystery is involved at these high points of the provision of God's mercy and grace. But it can be properly contemplated that God the Father looked on all the fallen mass of humanity, Adam and all his natural posterity, now lost to potential damnation and eternal perdition because of the demands of God's holy justice in response to their sin, and from them he elected some to redemption and eternal life. Why, it might be asked, did God not choose all to eternal life and forgiveness of sin? But the wonder of the grace of God is not that he failed to elect some to eternal life, but that he did, in fact, elect any. For all men, by reason of their participation in the guilt and entailment of Adam's sin, deserved nothing but God's wrath and curse.[6] None deserved his grace and mercy. His honor and his justice would have been vindicated had he left all of Adam's posterity to the eternal perdition their sin warranted. But God had mercy on some. The failure to grasp the meaning of what God has done resolves to a failure to grasp the seriousness of the state of sin, depravity, and inability to which all of Adam's posterity had fallen. The true meaning of sin explains both the necessity and the grace of God's predestinating election.

Against the reality of the Father's election, it was the redemptive office of God the Son to come into the world, to take human nature, yet without sin, into union with his divine nature, to give in that human nature a perfect obedience to the law of God as the substitute for the people whom the Father had given to him to redeem, and to bear the penalty for their sins

---

6. See Westminster Shorter Catechism, Question 84.

in his human nature by dying as their substitute. When we come in more detail to the redeeming work of Christ, we shall see that what we have just referred to as his redemptive office takes up his active obedience in keeping the law as our substitute, and his passive obedience in his death as our substitute. What was involved in the redemptive works of Christ, that is, will be more extensively explored when we consider what was involved in the divine purchase of salvation that our title has contemplated.

The redemptive office of the Holy Spirit is to apply to those for whom Christ died the benefits of the redemption that he accomplished. The Holy Spirit confers on them the gifts that Christ purchased for them in his death, notably the gifts of repentance and faith, joy in the Holy Spirit, peace of conscience, and perseverance to the end. The Holy Spirit's office is to call and sanctify those whom Christ has redeemed, to work sovereignly in their lives to conform them progressively to the image of holiness in Christ, and to conduct them to glory. "When he, the Spirit of truth is come," our Lord said, "he will guide you into all truth. . . He shall glorify me; for he shall receive of mine, and shall show it unto you" (John 16:13-14).

It is true that a strong dissent from the doctrine of God's election and predestination is made in some parts of the evangelical church. The claim is made, not that Christ died in the manner we have seen for a particular people, but for all people in general. That is to say, he bore the penalty of the guilt of all people. Such a claim involves not a *particular* but a general or a *universal* atonement. It will be necessary to return to that question when we consider the death and atonement of Christ more specifically. But it can be said in anticipation that the explanation for the claim of a general or universal atonement lies in a less than complete understanding of the biblical doctrine of our first parents' fall that brought sin into the world. The distinction of what we are here referring to as particular redemption (that is, the redemption of particular people), over against the error of assuming a general or universal redemption, is of such crucial importance for understanding what follows that a single text that has given rise to that false understanding can be noted.

Consider the apostle's statement in 1 John 2:2: "He (Christ) is the propitiation for our sins; and not for ours only, but also for the sins of the whole world." I well remember that some years ago a deacon in a church of which I was a member (the church was administered by a Board of Deacons, not by elders) said to me with somewhat of an air of finality when I revisited the church some years later: "If you don't hold to a universal atonement, what are you going to do with 1 John 2:2." Certainly, it might appear on the surface of things that by reason of its words, "the sins of the whole world," the text points to a general atonement as the fruits of the redemptive-atoning work of Christ. But such an understanding is not warranted, and an alternative view is not only possible but also necessary.

The statement at 1 John 2:2 is not to be understood as addressing the important question of the extent of the atonement. What is at issue in the text is the identity of the propitiator. That is to say, wherever, anywhere in the whole world, sins are propitiated, that is effected by the only competent propitiator in the plan of redemption that God has provided. Jesus Christ is the sole propitiator.

With the terms of the divine covenant of redemption in view, the important question arises as to how, in fact, the objectives of the decrees of God that were involved were to be realized. If, as has been claimed, God is the sovereign God of all history, if all that comes to pass eventuates according to the dictates of his will and the operation of his providence, what was necessary in order to bring to effect the redemption of those whom God, in the triune eternal council, had elected to salvation? We have spoken in earlier contexts of the covenant of works and of our first parent's repudiation of the obligations of that covenant that brought sin and death into the world. We have anticipated the fact that it was in order to discharge his people's liability under that covenant that the Second Person of the Godhead came into the world to become Jesus Christ and to give his life a ransom for them. Thus the need for redemption in actual history is made clear. How, then, was it to be realized?

The work of redemption is understandable, in the first place and at an initial level, in terms of what is referred to as the implementing covenant of common grace. By common grace, as distinguished from God's saving grace, is meant simply God's favor to his creatures in general. Though it is clear that "God is angry with the wicked every day" (Ps 7:11), nevertheless he loves his creatures as creatures. He showers his grace upon them, even though they do not acknowledge that all their good comes from God's gracious hands. At Matthew 5:45 we have it said that God the Father "makes his sun to rise on the evil and the good, and sendeth rain on the just and on the unjust." Such divine benevolence is at the heart of the meaning of common grace. God had formally and articulately established a covenant of common grace with Noah when he emerged from the ark. The details are well known. God said "I establish my covenant with you, and with your seed after you" (Gen 9:9).

Indeed, God's actions of benevolence and common grace had been operative from the very beginning. We recall that when our first parents sinned and were driven from the garden, "Unto Adam also and to his wife did the LORD God make coats of skins, and clothed them" (Gen 3:21). It is undoubtedly correct to understand that in that action of God, in the killing of the animals to provide the skins, we see the beginnings of the sacrificial system that came to explicit institution when the ceremonial law was given to Moses and was recorded in codified terms. But it may be suggested also that the action of God in thus providing covering and material comfort for our first parents was a divine action of common grace. The essence of the fall, we have observed, was Adam's false assertion of autonomy against God. Adam was, he claimed, competent to be his own judge and arbitrator of right and wrong, good and evil. He rejected God's criteria of the validity and truth in knowledge, and of action and behavior. He was sufficient to himself. But God, in the action of provision for him that we have noted, is saying that after, and because of, the fall man is unable to provide all necessities for himself. His imaginations of sovereignty are vacuous. God is saying that henceforth man will need God's provision for him. As God said to Noah, "I will remember my covenant, which is between me and you and every living creature" (Gen 9:15), stating that God will preserve the world that he had made for the benefit of man. The scriptural data are copious in instances of God's common grace. The Psalmist sums up aspects of it: "The LORD executeth judgment for the oppressed . . . giveth food to the hungry . . . raiseth them that are bowed down . . . relieveth the fatherless and widow" (Ps 146:7–9).

God's common grace can be seen to be operative in both a negative and a positive respect. First, in its negative aspect, common grace operates as a restraint of sin. Man is not, and does not become in this life, as evil as he could possibly be. At the crack of doom, when all individuals stand before the judgment seat of God, common grace will have come to an end, and in those who go to eternal perdition sin will come to its fullest expression. Second, in its positive aspect, common grace operates in the development of human culture and the process of human betterment. The achievements of science, the arts, and the human endowments that make such achievements possible are due to the operation of God's common grace.

## The Divine Purchase

But why does God's common grace continue? We are making these observations on common grace within the context of what is to be understood as the implementing covenants necessary to the realizations of what God has purposed in the covenant of redemption. The answer, then, to our present question is that God, who is the Lord of history, operates providentially in the world by his common grace for, among other things, a vital reason. That is that the world will be preserved until all those whom God gave to his Son to redeem have heard the gospel, have been brought by the Holy Spirit of God to repentance and saving faith in Christ, and the full complement of the kingdom of God has been realized. Then the crack of doom will come.

In order to realize the objectives of the covenant of redemption it was necessary that in such ways an arrangement, or a series of arrangements, to accomplish that end must be instituted within the time process in which we exist. For that purpose, what we now refer to as the covenant of grace came into existence. God having sovereignly elected to eternal life the subjects of the covenant of redemption, he now, in terms of the covenant of grace, entered into a covenant with them to bring them by certain means and processes to eternal life with himself. The parties to the covenant were, then, God the Father on the one hand, and his elect people on the other. Or more particularly, God established the covenant between himself and his people *as represented by Christ*. Christ came into the world as the Lord of the covenant. He represented his people in all of the aspects of his redemptive work, in his satisfying the demands of God's law in his active obedience, and in his substitutionary death of the cross on their behalf.

Christ's coming into the world made possible the fulfillment of God's promise that the time would come when he would establish a new covenant with his people. All of the types and foreshadowings of the old Mosaic covenant would be fulfilled in the antitype, the Lord Jesus Christ. "This shall be the covenant that I will make with the house of Israel; After those days, saith the LORD, I will put my law in their inward parts, and write it in their hearts; and will be their God, and they shall be my people" (Jer 31:33). That glorious consummation turned on Christ's coming into the world and identifying himself with his people and their necessities. The reference to "the house of Israel" in that statement is to be carefully understood. Paul the apostle has it at Romans 9:6 that "They are not all Israel, which are of Israel." Not all of natural and national Israel will be saved and enter the kingdom of God. When God terminated his special relation with Israel of old a new

Israel, a spiritual Israel, came into being. For as we shall see in the following chapter, as a result of Christ's redemptive work the doors of the kingdom of God were thrown wide open to the Gentiles, and the conclusion rests that "If ye be Christ's, then are ye Abraham's seed, and heirs according to the promise" (Gal 3:29). The estrangement between Israel and the Gentiles was abolished, God has "broken down the middle wall of partition" (Eph 2:14), and henceforth there is one church in which Jews and Gentiles are "all one in Christ Jesus" (Gal 3:28).

In all of God's covenants there are contained both promises and obligations, the scope and import of which need to be kept in view. We have seen that clearly contained in the covenant that God made with Adam was a precise obligation. Adam was to refrain from eating of the forbidden tree and he was to perform certain acts of obedience to the law that God had promulgated to him. The promise of that initial covenant was that in response to his obedience, Adam would have been rewarded with eternal life. Now within the terms of the covenant of grace, both obligations and promises apply. We shall see those obligations and promises working out more fully when we consider in the following chapter the work of Christ as the sinner's substitute for salvation. But a number of relevant points can be anticipated at this stage.

First, when it is said that the justification of the repentant sinner in the sight of God turns simply on his faith in Jesus Christ and the atonement for sin that Christ has made, the question arises whether the covenant of grace is in any sense a conditional covenant. For under the covenant of grace, "a man is not justified by the works of the law, but by the faith of [in] Jesus Christ, even as we have believed in Jesus Christ, that we might be justified by the faith of [in] Christ, and not by the works of the law; for by the works of the law shall no flesh be justified" (Gal 2:16). Certainly no condition for salvation can be met and fulfilled by the sinner. The covenant of grace accordingly cannot be construed to be conditional on the sinner's part. But at that point the glory of the gospel enters. The entire covenantal arrangement required that Christ, the Lord of the covenant, must fulfill certain conditions on the sinner's behalf. Again there comes into view, therefore, the divinely-stated requirement that Christ must fulfill completely and meticulously all that had been required of the people he represented. He must fulfill God's law perfectly. He must pay to the full satisfaction of God the Father the penalty due to the people he represented for their having broken God's law.

## The Divine Purchase

Our Lord perfectly fulfilled all of the obligations which, under the covenant of grace, he sustained on our behalf. But what of the promises under the covenant of grace? A careful reading of the scriptural data makes it clear that God the Father's promises to his Son were to the effect that, on the Son's fulfilling all of the requirements of the covenant of grace, he would be rewarded in the manner that is now observable in the scriptural text. First, when he had lived his perfect and sinless life on our behalf and he could say to the Father "I have finished the work which thou gavest me to do" (John 17:4), he could request of the Father, "Now, O Father, glorify thou me with thine own self with the glory which I had with thee before the world was" (John 17:5). And on the grounds of his faithfulness the Father responded in precisely corresponding terms: "When he had by himself purged our sins, [he] sat down on the right hand of the Majesty on high" (Heb 1:3). And being "obedient unto death, even the death of the cross . . . God also hath highly exalted him, and given him a name that is above every name" (Phil 2:8–9). On those grounds, the promises of eternal life accrue to the Christian believer by reason of the satisfaction that Christ offered to the Father by his fulfilling the obligations of the covenant of grace. And further, the believer shares also, as a result, in the blessings of fellowship with God the Father and the Son that the Holy Spirit of God conveys to him in this life.

The ways in which God has implemented the covenant of grace in history are revealed in successive forms of its administration in, first, God's initial covenant with Abraham; second, the covenant with his people given through Moses; and third, the inauguration, as has been seen, of the "new covenant" in and by Christ. Abraham, Moses, and Christ—the parts they play in the fulfillment of God's of gracious purpose illuminate the course of human history and the resolution to which it moves.

The administration of the covenant of grace that was instituted by God's calling of Abraham spans across history from that early time until the coming of Christ. Some four hundred and thirty years after the establishment of the covenant with Abraham, as Paul says to the Galatians (Gal 3:17), God gave the law to Moses and thereby instituted a new form of administration. But as Paul stated to the Galatians, the terms of God's covenant with Abraham were not in any sense altered or abrogated by what was subsequently established at the time of Moses. The covenant with Abraham continued unchanged through the Mosaic administration. So that, nestling within the covenant with Abraham, which arches through time from Abraham to Christ, is the covenant with Moses. The Mosaic covenant extends to the coming of Christ.

Christ came as our "great high priest" (Heb 4:14) and as the antitype of all of the types of the Mosaic administration, and his coming was the fulfillment of the initial promise God gave to Abraham. The "new covenant" (Jer 31:31–33) that Christ inaugurated is then the restatement in a new form of administration of the covenant of grace, in terms of which God has sworn to redeem his people and bring them to glory.

God's promise to Abraham was threefold. He promised him, first, that a great nation would descend from him and that in him, by means of what God would do through his natural and spiritual descendants, many nations would be blessed; second, a land that his descendants would occupy at a precise stage of their history, a promise that was completely fulfilled, as recorded in Joshua 21:43–45: "The LORD gave unto Israel all the land which he sware to give unto their fathers. . . . There failed not ought of any good thing which the LORD had spoken unto the house of Israel; all came to pass"; third, that God would be God to the people whom he would make the beneficiaries of the covenantal promises. The culminating and the very precious aspect of God's promise was that he would be God to his people.

In order to establish those covenantal promises in a manner in which they could be understood and grasped and depended on, God swore an oath of faithfulness. "God, willing more abundantly to show unto the heirs of promise the immutability of his counsel confirmed it by an oath" (Heb 6:17). The preceding text at Hebrews 6:14 refers explicitly to God's confirmation of promise as it was given to Abraham on the occasion of Abraham's willingness to offer his son Isaac as a sacrifice (Gen 22:2, 17). But we reflect also on God's having sworn an oath of faithfulness on an earlier occasion when he instructed Abraham to take certain animals and, having killed them, to divide them into parts that he was to lay side by side. Then God, in the form of a burning lamp, passed between the divided parts in a manner that was common to the ratification of covenants at that time in history. The oath that God swore in doing so was his oath of faithfulness to the terms of the covenant. It was his oath of self-malediction. God was saying by that action that if he was not faithful to what he had promised, then let him not be God.

It is at that point that the glory of the gospel appears. The promises of God's successive covenants were those of benediction in response to obedience, and malediction in response to disobedience. The promise of malediction must be followed by the wrath and curse of God and the imposition of penalty in response to sin by those individuals who were parties to the covenant. If the latter were not so, the justice and honor of God would be violated. When we take full account of the outcomes of the covenantal administration and promises, it is all too clear that on man's part the curse of malediction was warranted. And as history shows, the curse of malediction did fall, and it fell with all the weight of the wrath of God. But it fell, not on individuals who warranted the curse by reason of their sin. It fell on the One whom God the Father sent to be the substitute for those whom he had chosen to redeem. When God's people were thus exposed to the curse, they were redeemed because, as Paul wrote to the Galatians, "Christ hath redeemed us from the curse of the law, being made a curse for us" (Gal 3:13).

The Mosaic administration, which extended until the coming of Christ, contained an elaborate system of ceremonial arrangements associated with the tabernacle and later the temple, the sacrificial system, and the priestly phenomena. They formed a temporary or typical and anticipatory order, looking forward to the coming of Christ. The time would come when God would terminate his special relation with his people Israel in order that the kingdom of Christ could be established in its widest and most conclusive extent. Christ would come as the antitype of all the types of him included in the older administrations of the covenant of grace. Then the doors of the kingdom, as has been anticipated, would be thrown wide open to the Gentiles. The inclusion of the Gentiles in the kingdom of God was anticipated in the record concerning Melchisedek (Gen 14:18), Rahab (Jos 2:3; Heb 11:31), and Ruth (Ruth 1:16), and in the ministry of our Lord (John 4:7; Matt 15:22–28). The letter to the Hebrews is an extended exposition of the manner in which Christ came as the perfect high priest and fulfilled all the promises contained in the types, notably the Levitical priesthood, that had anticipated and pointed to him.

Many aspects of the Mosaic administration anticipated the coming of Christ. Paramount within it, among the many sacrifices that were offered daily and on other special occasions, was the sacrifice made for sin on the annual Day of Atonement (Lev 16). On that day the high priest first offered a sacrifice for his own sin and then, having by that means acquired ceremonial holiness for himself, he offered a sacrifice for the sins of the people. He was permitted and required on that single day of the year to enter the most holy place within the tabernacle and sprinkle the blood of the sacrifice on the Ark of the Covenant and the mercy seat.

But the blood of bulls and goats could not take away sin. It could not provide a definitive atonement that would deal not only with the ceremonial guilt of the people but with the moral guilt that separated them from God. It was necessary that Christ should come as our "great high priest" to deal with sin by his once-for-all sacrifice of himself. Christ faithfully discharged his earthly high priestly office and he returned to heaven and now discharges his heavenly high priestly office on our behalf. In that, he ever lives to make intercession for us (Heb 7:25).

Before us now, having looked at the covenantal structure of God's decree and accomplishment of redemption, is the question of precisely how the terms and promises of the covenants were actually fulfilled by the saving work of Christ. We turn to that immediately in the following chapter.

CHAPTER 4

# The Divine Personhood of Christ

Following his resurrection, our Lord showed himself to his disciples "being seen of them forty days, and speaking of the things pertaining to the kingdom of God" (Acts 1:3). Here was the beginning of new conceptions in the disciples' minds, new levels of apprehension of who this person was with whom they had traveled for so long and of what he had come into the world to do. He had recognized their emotional anxiety and their sorrow when, before his crucifixion, he told them that it was necessary that he should leave them. They had journeyed with him, they had seen his works of mercy, and they had witnessed his healing the sick and even raising the dead. They had seen him weary and languishing in human spirit from the burdens of ministry that he took upon himself. And they had witnessed his escape to seclusion and his spending whole nights in prayer; so much so that they asked him one day to teach them to pray also (Luke 11:1). But they had understood him only imperfectly.

One, whom Christ himself chose as a closest of friends, had leaned on his breast at the final supper he had with them on the night on which he was betrayed. That disciple, John, together with Peter and James had been with him when, on the Mount of Transfiguration, they saw him with Moses and Elijah transfigured in glory. But they slept on that mountain that day. They would do so again when, before his final arrest on trumped-up charges on that Gethsemane night, he agonized alone as the weight of what lay ahead bore on his human soul. Surely he was the Son of God, they had thought on occasion. Peter, ever the forthright spokesman among them, had answered our Lord when he asked, "Whom say ye that I am," by replying, "Thou art the Christ, the Son of the living God" (Matt 16:15–16). Peter had made that confession, Christ said, by the revelation of the Father (Matt 16:17). But even so, Peter's faith faltered. We know of his fall, his regret, his repentance, and his rehabilitation. Our Lord had warned the disciples of Satan's desires against them, and for reasons that were to become clear in the sequel, he prayed explicitly for Peter (Luke 22:31–32, noting the singular pronoun in the Greek text when our Lord said to Peter, "I have prayed for thee"). On the occasion on which our Lord gave his remarkable discourse on his identity as the bread of life, he recognized that many did not believe on him, and he took encouragement from his divine awareness that "All that the Father giveth me shall come to me" (John 6:37). But he pointedly asked his disciples, "Will ye also go away?" Again Peter replied: "Lord, to whom shall we go? thou hast the words of eternal life" (John 6:67–68).

But the disciples understood only imperfectly. Grieved that their Lord had said to them, "It is expedient for you that I go away" (John 16:7), they were comforted by his promise, though it was not clearly understood, that "I will not leave you comfortless. I will come to you" (John 14:18). At the conclusion of his Galilean ministry, when he "stedfastly set his face to go to Jerusalem" and to his sacrificial death (Luke 9:51), he said clearly that "The Son of man must suffer many things . . . and be slain and be raised the third day" (Luke 9:22). And now, in the forty days between his resurrection and his ascension to the Father, he came again to speak to them of all that pertained to the very reason for his coming into the world. It had to do with "the kingdom of God" (Acts 1:3), the meaning of that kingdom in the context of God's eternal redemptive purpose, the part the disciples were to play in furthering its extent in the world, and his further assurance that he would be with them as they discharged their commission, "even unto the end of the world" (Matt 28:20).

At that time, our Lord said two things to his disciples by way of assurance and direction. First, he "commanded them that they should not depart from Jerusalem, but wait for the promise of the Father . . . ye shall be baptized with the Holy Ghost not many days hence" (Acts 1:4–5). That promise was fulfilled on the Day of Pentecost when the disciples, not drunk with new wine (Acts 2:13) as the credulous crowd had imagined, but moved by the Holy Spirit, preached in various languages the good news of the gospel. The promise of Christ that he would come to them was fulfilled. He came again to dwell with them by his Holy Spirit. The reality of what had been the benefit of the disciples' regeneration came to highly explicit self-consciousness. Christ was with them. They were joined in union with him. He lived in them and they in him (see Gal 2:20). Now their "fellowship with the Father and with his Son Jesus Christ," of which the beloved apostle

John was subsequently to speak at greater length (see 1 John 1:3), was to be the determining and formative blessing of their lives.

Second, in his post-resurrection appearances to his disciples, Christ explained to them that "Ye shall receive power, after that the Holy Ghost is come upon you; and ye shall be witnesses unto me both in Jerusalem, and in all Judea, and in Samaria, and unto the uttermost part of the earth" (Acts 1:8). The early chapters of the Acts contain the history of that gradual spreading of the gospel through Judea and Samaria. And then, as the church expanded and the history blossomed, the gospel was carried to the extended parts of the world. Most notably in the missionary journeys of Paul, first with Barnabas and then with Silas, Timothy and others at various stages, the gospel of salvation was spread.

On his return to Jerusalem from his third missionary journey which had taken him through Macedonia to Athens and Corinth, Paul stopped at the seaport of Miletus on the western coast of Asia and from there he called the elders of the church at nearby Ephesus to meet with him. That meeting is of singular importance in the history of the early church. Paul there charged the elders to remember diligently their responsibility as "overseers" of "the church of God, which he hath purchased with his own blood" (Acts 20:28). In that single sentence Paul effectively addressed the twofold question that engages us: "Who is Jesus Christ"? And "Why did Jesus Christ come into the world?" The answers lie at the heart of God's revelation of the gospel. First, Paul's statement says, Jesus Christ is God. He is eternally God in his own right. And second, Jesus Christ came into the world to purchase the church with his own blood. The church was purchased by the human blood of God. Eternity will not exhaust the Christian's wonder and praise as he plumbs the depth of the meaning of that remarkable event.

Those conclusions acquire their meaning because they reflect the covenantal structure of God's redemptive purpose, as we looked at that in the preceding chapter. The redeemer, the only mediator between God and man, was not always Jesus Christ. He was the eternal Second Person of the Godhead who came into the world to become Jesus Christ. He came as the antitype of all of the types in the earlier administration of God's covenant of grace that had anticipated and pointed to him. He came to satisfy the demands of God's judgment of wrath against the sins of his people and, as the apostle Peter encapsulates it, to "bear our sins in his own body on the tree, that we, being dead to sins, should live unto righteousness; by whose stripes ye were healed" (1 Pet 2:24). There precisely is the fulfillment of Isaiah's

## The Divine Personhood of Christ

prophecy, which so brilliantly captured in economic terms the remarkable substitution that was involved: "*He* was wounded for *our* transgressions, *he* was bruised for *our* iniquities; the chastisement of *our* peace was upon *him*; and with *his* stripes *we* are healed" (Isa 53:5). The "Lord of glory" (1 Cor 2:8) "being in the form of God . . . was made in the likeness of men and . . . humbled himself and became obedient unto death, even the death of the cross" (Phil 2:6–8). We face the mystery of all the ages, that one who was God, very God of very God as the Nicene Creed appropriately states it, should become man.

In an earlier age, at the turn of the eleventh century, the worthy theologian, Anselm, Archbishop of Canterbury, asked the question in his book, *Cur Deus Homo* (Why did God become man?). In that, centuries before the Reformation theology expanded the answer, he articulated what became referred to as the satisfaction theory of our Lord's atonement. Anselm's discussion and answer focused on the need to preserve the honor of God. It would be expanded in subsequent Reformed theology. But in it all, in addressing the important question of why God in Christ became man, we hold with doctrinal tenacity and theological truth that Jesus Christ was truly God. We hold, on the grounds not only of the church's dogma, but of scriptural data, that he was not a human person. He was, he remained when he was in this world, a divine Person. He continues for all eternity a divine Person in the human nature he assumed for our salvation.

The personhood of Christ lies at the very foundation of all truth related to the salvation of God's elect. It is for that reason that early heresies that attacked the church and the formalization of biblical truth repeatedly focused on attacking the person of Christ. If Satan could abolish from men's minds the truth of the personhood of Christ who had come as the redeemer he would have won the day. Without Christ there is no Christianity. Christianity is not simply a religion of moral rectitude. Morality in and of itself is not Christianity. The key to the very meaning of Christianity is Christ, and what he has done in his human nature to reconcile sinful people to God. Without him there is no redemption from sin. Without Christ the world is still in satanically enshrouded darkness. Moreover, it is not simply the *teaching* of Christ that provides the foundation and establishes the superstructure of Christianity. It is the *Person* of Christ that distinguishes Christianity from all other systems of thought. Take away the founders of other systems and the structure of thought may remain. We may have Kantian philosophy without Kant, Arminianism as a system of theology without Arminius. That is because their significance centers in what they taught, not in who or what they were. But that is not so with Christianity. Christianity is what it is because, in his Person, Jesus Christ is who he is.

As early as the apostolic times, the doctrine of the person of Christ was attacked by various heretical claims that went under the general name of Gnosticism. The Greek word underlying that name, γνῶσις, *gnōsis*, means knowledge, and Gnosticism claimed essentially that there existed higher forms of knowledge than ordinary men and presumed Christians were able to attain to. Gnosticism held that a distinction existed between the spiritual and the material in the sense that what was material was evil, contrary to what was spiritually good. For that reason there could not be any mixture of the spiritual and the material. It followed in that system of thought that there could not therefore exist a person, as the Christians claimed the Son of God to be, who was both divine and human. Gnosticism in its many expressions was essentially a heresy that denied the reality of the deity and divinity of Christ. Some forms of the teaching, such as a related form known as Docetism, argued that Jesus Christ possessed only a phantom body, and others argued that he was only an ordinary man to whom and on whom the Spirit of God came at an early point of his life, but that the Spirit left him at his crucifixion.

The church's doctrine was soon under attack from other developed sources. A form of false teaching known as Arianism claimed that Christ was a created entity, created by God and entrusted with certain assignments such as the creation of the world, but that he was not himself eternally God. The Arian heresy was rejected decisively by the council of the church at Nicea in the year 325, and the worthy Athanasius defended the decision of that council forcibly in the years that followed. The heresy of Sabellianism also arose in the early centuries and argued that what the Christians referred to as the second and third Persons of the Trinity, God the Son, and God the Holy Spirit, did not exist as distinguishable Persons within the trinity of the Godhead, but were simply emanations of the one God. The Council of Constantinople in 381 confirmed the deliverances of the Nicean Council. What has come down to us as the Nicene Creed is properly referred to as the Niceno-Constantinopolitan Creed. The church's doctrine of the Person of Christ was finally settled in dogmatic form at the Council of Chalcedon in the year 451. It was stated there that Jesus Christ was one divine Person in whom two natures, the divine and the human, were joined in union "without confusion, without change, without division, and

## The Divine Personhood of Christ

without separation." The first two of those defining characteristics established that the two natures were separate in the sense that there was no communication of properties between them. The divine nature remained divine and the human nature remained human, without any properties of the one being transferred to, or being partaken of by the other. The last two of the defining characteristics established that the union of natures was a real and actual union.

The meaning of that so-called Christological settlement in the Chalcedonian dogma is that in Jesus Christ as he walked in this world there were two minds, a divine and a human, two capacities of affection, a divine and a human, and a divine and a human will. That followed from the fact that, by reason of his incarnation, Christ possessed a full human nature, with all the capacities and abilities of the faculties of human soul, intellectual, affective, and volitional. That, moreover, has profound significance for the meaning of all that Christ did in this world. Most notably, in the same way as he kept the law of God perfectly in his human nature, he also died in his human nature. He could not die in his divine nature. He had subjected himself to temptation in his human nature. Satan could not tempt him in his divine nature. Satan did once attempt to do that, and he was cast out of heaven as a result. Then beyond his having prevailed over Satan throughout his human life, a proper construal of Christ's suffering in his substitutionary death is necessary. He died in his human nature. In his doing so, the full faculties of his humanity were involved and he suffered in human soul and in human body.

But the biblical doctrine of the personhood of Christ requires a further significant conclusion. By reason of his incarnation, it follows that as to his human nature he was in the world, while as to his divine nature he was both in this world and in heaven. At one point of his ministry he referred to himself as "The Son of man which is in heaven" (John 3:13). While it is recognized that that phrase does not appear in all Greek manuscripts, its statement can be adequately supported on biblical grounds.[1] Now, by reason of his ascension back to the Father, as to his human nature he is in heaven, while as to his divine nature he is both in heaven and in the world.

Mystery attaches to the incarnation of Christ. It was not the case that God created *ex nihilo*, a fetus for implantation in the womb of the virgin. Christ was born of the substance of the virgin and therefore took possession of a full human nature, yet without sin. The miracle of the incarnation was therefore twofold. First, there was a breaking of the entailment of sin.

---

1. See the relevant argument in Hendriksen, *Commentary*, 2:500–501.

## The Divine Purchase

The angel answered Mary's "How shall this be" with the remarkable words, "The Holy Ghost shall come upon thee, and the power of the Highest shall overshadow thee; therefore also that holy thing which shall be born of thee shall be called the Son of God" (Luke 1:35). A judicious Puritan commentator, Matthew Poole, finds in that statement not only that the Holy Spirit would impregnate the womb of the mother, but that the birth would be "of thy flesh *first sanctified*."[2] That is to say, the entailment of sin was broken at that point and the child that was born was completely without the taint of sin. The second aspect of the mystery and miracle of incarnation was the Holy Spirit's impregnation of the egg of the mother.

Why was it necessary that the redeemer who thus came into the world should be both human and divine? Sin had entered the world in human nature (Rom 5:12), and it followed that the righteous justice of God must be satisfied by a perfect fulfillment of his law in human nature. At the same time it was necessary that the penalty for our having broken the law of God must be paid in human nature. But no mere man could perform those necessary functions. No man could be a salvific substitute for men. Every man was liable to eternal perdition for his own sin. If any from among the fallen host of Adam and his natural posterity were to be saved, a substitute redeemer must come from outside the realm of humanity. He must be sinless in his own right in order that not having to pay a penalty for his own sin, he could bear the penalty of the sins of others. He must be a human substitute, as has been said, by reason of the necessity that the wrath of God attracted by the human default of sin must be propitiated in human nature. The only alternative available was that God himself, in the Person of his Son, should come into the world and do what his holy justice demanded should be done for man's redemption. That answered Anselm's *Cur Deus Homo*, why God became man. The Son of God came into the world because there was no other way in which the honor of God in his eternal holiness and righteousness could be preserved. The redeemer must be divine because no mere man could bear the blaze of the wrath of God against sin that the mediator between God and man had necessarily to bear. Indeed, it was by the support of the Holy Spirit that Christ "offered himself without spot to God" (Heb 9:14).

The Second Person of the Godhead assumed to himself, then, a created (by incarnation), temporal, and finite human nature. In his entering into the process of time that he himself had created, the eternal and the

---

2. Poole, *Commentary*, 190, italics added.

temporal were brought into a new relation. But the eternal and the temporal could not be commingled and confused. They remained separate and unimpaired in their respective relevancies. The process of redemption was actually played out in historical time. The atonement that accomplished our redemption was a real-time, definite, historical atonement. Moreover, in the same way as there was no commingling of the eternal and the temporal at the incarnation, neither was there any such commingling at the atonement that Christ provided for sin. Again, no commingling could occur at the point at which the sinner is translated by the work of God from the kingdom of darkness into the kingdom of his dear Son (Col 1:13). That is because, first, our salvation, the Scriptures make clear, is all of grace. It is by the grace of God that we are saved (Eph 2:8). It is God himself who makes his Son to be unto us "wisdom and righteousness and sanctification and redemption" (1 Cor 1:30). Only by the sovereign grace of God, reaching from eternity beyond the createdness of time in which we are bound, are we rescued from the ignorance, guilt, pollution, and misery of sin.

The point may be made differently. In the sinner's transference from wrath to grace at the point of his regeneration, there is again no commingling of the eternal and the temporal. Regeneration is entirely the work of God's Spirit in and on the very recesses of the soul. It is entirely the work of God's grace and in it the individual has no part at all. We shall say at a later point that regeneration is the secret, sovereign, and unsolicited work of God's divine Spirit. If we were to claim to the contrary, as do some current theologies, and say that the individual plays a part in his regeneration, we would be saying that the temporal, man's assumed part, is commingled with the eternal, the operative grace of God. We would be erroneously contemplating a joint activity of the grace of God on the one hand and human merit and effort on the other.

When we say that by the incarnation of Christ eternity and time have been brought into a new relation, we are referring to a relation that will continue throughout the eternal age. For having assumed a temporal human nature into union with himself, our Lord has not divested himself of it. Now in his mysterious supervision of the becoming as well as the being of his redeemed people, God by his works of providence and the ministry of his Spirit is also immanent in historical time to bring us to glory.

In coming into the world and partaking of our full, though sinless, humanity, our Lord did not cease to be God. He did not lay aside his glory, though he did set aside the signs or insignia of his glory. He was, we have said, a divine person. He did not become a human person. Nor is it to be said that he was a divine-human person. The meaning of such a latter claim would be that he was a person in whom the divine and the human natures were commingled or blended together in a manner that, by virtue of their interfusion and interpenetration, rendered it impossible to say that he was either uniquely divine or uniquely human.

It has been a common misunderstanding of the Person of our Lord to claim that when he came into the world he did, in some sense, lay aside his divine attributes. Such a teaching might appear to be supported by the paragraph in the second chapter of Paul's letter to the Philippians on which it is supposedly based. Our Lord, as Paul says there, "made himself of no reputation, and took upon him the form of a servant, and was made in the likeness of men; and being found in fashion as a man, he humbled himself" (Phil 2:7–8). Where the text says "made himself of no reputation" the Greek text has the word ἐκένωσεν, *ekenōsen*, which means, literally, poured out or emptied himself. It is from the Greek word that the teaching we have referred to, known as the "kenotic" theory, derives its claim. But the Philippian passage does not bear such an interpretation. The English language text is plainly concerned with the manner in which the Second Person of the Godhead humbled himself in order that he might be our redeemer.

The letter to the Hebrews focuses our thought on the identity of Christ as our great high priest. But it is Christ *incarnate* who is presented to us in that office. It is the incarnate Christ who lived and died for us and who, by his active and passive obedience, purchased a title to heaven for us. It was in his human nature that he died and rose again. It was in his human nature that he ascended and sits "at the right hand of the Majesty on high" (Heb 1:3). It is in his human nature that he makes intercession for us, and it is in his human nature that he is coming again to receive us to himself.

It is true that many aspects of the life and experiences and actions of our Lord that are uniquely attributable to his human nature (for example, "Jesus wept" [John 11:35]) are attributed in the Scriptures to his person. Similarly, actions that are as clearly referable to his divine nature are attributed to his person. But in all its uniqueness and individual identity, Christ's personhood was determined essentially by his divine nature. The divine nature dominated and determined and controlled the human nature.

As to the *Person* of Jesus Christ, we say that he was impeccable. Impeccability means "impossible to sin." We do not say that the human nature of Christ, considered in and of itself as a human nature, was impeccable.

## The Divine Personhood of Christ

Conceivably, if left to itself as an isolated human nature, it may have been capable of sin. For the temptations of Christ, tempted "in all points like as we are" (Heb 4:15), were real temptations. Indeed, the assaults of Satan upon him in his human nature constituted our Lord's probation, to be contemplated in comparison with the probation under which Adam was placed at the beginning. For the first Adam was a type of the second (see Rom 5:14; 1 Cor 15:45, 47). But what our Lord's human nature may have been capable of, in and of itself, it was not capable of when it was joined with the divine nature in the divine Person of Christ. It was the *Person* of Christ that was impeccable.

In his human nature, Christ knew and thought and willed and suffered as a man. In his human nature, as the writer to the Hebrews states, he "learned obedience by the things which he suffered" in order that, "being made perfect, he became the author of eternal salvation unto all them that obey him" (Heb 5:8–9). Indeed, his suffering in the flesh qualified him to serve as our high priest and, in that office, to give himself a ransom for sin.

What has been said to this point of the Personhood of Christ turns on his eternal identity as the Second Person of the Godhead. Mystery attaches to the doctrine and reality of the divine Trinity, and in anticipation of what is said further of the Person of Christ it will be useful to note the following conclusion on that doctrine by the twentieth-century Reformed theologian, L. Berkhof. As to the eternal generation of the Son, Berkhof states: "It is that eternal and necessary act of the first person in the Trinity, whereby He, within the divine being, is the ground of a second personal subsistence like His own, and puts this second person in possession of the whole divine essence, without any division, alienation, or change."[3] Berkhof continues in similar terms, relating to the procession of the Holy Spirit from the Father and the Son. That may be defined as "that eternal and necessary act of the first and second persons in the Trinity whereby they, within the divine Being, become the ground of the personal subsistence of the Holy Spirit, and put the third person in possession of the whole divine essence, without any division, alienation or change."[4]

What is being said is that, in timeless eternity, God the Son proceeded from the Father, and that God the Holy Spirit proceeded from the Father and the Son. The relevant body of doctrine, which it is not necessary to consider at further length for our present purposes, deserves extensive

---

3. Berkhof, *Systematic Theology*, 94.
4. Ibid., 97.

investigation. But reflecting now on our present comments on the divine identity of Christ, we say that he is eternally God in his own right. As is true of the Holy Spirit also, on the grounds of what has been said, he is autotheotic. The word means that he is God in his own right. That means that, as to his nature, he is eternally God, while as to his person, he is of the Father. That is, he was begotten of the Father. In his distinguishable personhood (distinguishable in that he is eternally begotten) he is one in substance with the Father and the Holy Spirit, such that the full essence of the Godhead resides in him. He, with the Father and the Holy Spirit, participated in what we have referred to as the determinate council of the Godhead before the foundation of the world. As the apostle John states in the prologue to his gospel, he was "in the beginning with God, and he (the Word) was God [and] all things were made by him" (see John 1:1–3). Paul states similarly to the Colossians that he is "the image of the invisible God . . . [and] by him were all things created" (Col 1:15–16). In the eternal deliberations of the Godhead, Christ in his eternal identity spoke forth the very law of God to which, in his incarnation, he voluntarily made himself subject in this world. Such is the mystery of redemption, or, as Paul has it in his letter to Timothy, "Great is the mystery of godliness" (1 Tim 3:16). And the mystery that the apostle has in view at that point is precisely that of the fact that "God (in Christ) was manifest in the flesh." Well has Charles Wesley said in his hymn, "Veiled in flesh the Godhead see; / Hail th'incarnate deity."[5]

What, finally, is to be said of the coming into the world of Christ, the eternal Son of God? We shall explore the purpose of his coming further in the following chapter, when we consider more closely what we have referred to as the divine purchase. We shall see the humiliation to which the Son of God voluntarily submitted himself. The hymn writer, John Henry Newman, captured the meaning in a sentence: "O loving wisdom of our God! / When all was sin and shame / A second Adam to the fight / And to the rescue came."[6]

---

5. Wesley, "Hark! The herald angels sing . . ." in *Congregational Praise*, 84, and various hymnals.

6. Newman, "Praise to the Holiest in the height . . ." in ibid., 71, and various hymnals.

CHAPTER 5

# The Divine Purchase

THE STATEMENT OF PAUL the apostle to the Ephesian elders that "God purchased the church with his own blood" (Acts 20:28) clearly implied, as we saw in the preceding chapter, the full deity as well as the full humanity of Christ who made the offering for sin. We turn now to reflect on the fact that Christ *purchased* the church. That was what we are referring to as the divine purchase. For in the atonement for sin, it was necessary that, in response to the demands of God's holy justice, the price of a penalty for sins that had been committed must be paid.

Christ purchased the salvation of his people, those whom, before the foundation of the world, the Father gave to him to redeem. Our confessional standards observe in expansive terms that "The liberty which Christ hath purchased for believers under the gospel consists in their freedom from the guilt of sin, the condemning wrath of God, the curse of the moral law; and in their being delivered from this present evil world, bondage to Satan, and dominion of sin . . . and everlasting damnation"[1] The confessional statement is worthy of more complete citation and examination. The result of the saving work of Christ as exhibited is that "There is therefore now no condemnation to them which are in Christ Jesus" (Rom 8:1); and "Being justified by faith, we have peace with God through our Lord Jesus Christ" (Rom 5:1). God is now at peace with his people. By virtue of the substitutionary atonement that he has provided in his Son, his justice has been satisfied and he is "just, and the justifier of him which believeth in Jesus" (Rom 3:26).

---

1. *Westminster Confession of Faith* (1647), chapter XX:1. The same statement is made in the *Savoy Declaration of Faith* (1658), chapter XXI, and the *Second London (Baptist) Confession* (1689), chapter XXI.

## The Divine Purchase

Here we have coming into focus what has been referred to in doctrinal theological terms as the "ransom theory" of the atonement. That terminology is intended to reflect the claims that Christ himself had made. "The Son of man came," he said, "to give his life a ransom for many" (Mark 10:45; Matt 20:28). The purchase involved in providing that ransom is clearly displayed in the Scriptures. Paul made the point to the Corinthian church: "Ye are *bought* with a price" (1 Cor 6:20, 7:23). Peter refers to certain false teachers whose "damnable heresies" denied "the Lord that *bought* them" (2 Pet 2:1). The Psalmist prays to God to remember his people "which thou hast *purchased*" (Ps 74:2). Transferring the conception from the Old to the New Testament, or, as has been noted, from the old to the new form of administration of God's covenant of grace, Paul refers to those whom Christ has redeemed as his "*purchased* possession" (Eph 1:14).

That God purchased his own people, as the Psalmist has stated, in the Old Testament times should not be seen as completely distinct from what God has done in the Person of his Son in the newer dispensation. For it is a truth inherent in all of God's administrations that he has never had any dealings with man except through his Son. God's bountiful acts of common grace are administered only by reason that, first, it is by his Son that he upholds the world and works out its destiny and spreads liberally his gifts to men (Col 1:15–17). And second, while not all of God's people of old, the nation-church of Israel, were numbered among his elect, for "they are not all Israel, which are of Israel" (Rom 9:6), it is true that those who did believe the promise that the redeemer would come were regenerate because the saving benefits of Christ's atonement were communicated to them by the Holy Spirit.

But the word, or the concept, of purchase has not appeared in all recent translations of the Scriptures. Some have preferred to say, with reference to Paul's statement at Acts 20:28, that the church was "obtained" by the blood of Christ. Of course, in the totality of his piacular work, Christ "obtained" the church. But the question arises whether, in the light of larger contextual considerations, a "purchase" rather than an "obtaining" was operative in the redemptive-messianic work of our Lord.

We may note that in Acts 20:28 the Greek word περιεποιήσατο, *periepoiēsato*, which is in a special Greek form that refers to an action performed once-for-all at a specific time, has been translated as "purchased" in certain interlinear translations. Those include the earlier nineteenth-century

## The Divine Purchase

work of George Ricker Berry,[2] and the recent translation by R. K. Brown and P. W. Comfort.[3] Other interlinear translations use such words as "acquired"[4] and "procured."[5] The relevant Greek word, as already referred to, is common to the different manuscripts underlying the King James Version and the English Standard Version translations. The standard Greek lexicon (Bauer, Arndt, and Gingrich) references the text we are at present addressing as sustaining the meaning of περιεποιήσατο, *periepoiēsato*, as to "acquire, obtain, gain for oneself."[6] It is clear, then, that in view of these variations of translation, it is necessary to reflect on the larger contextual meaning of the relevant text and its significance for the doctrine of the atonement. What in fact was involved in the saving work of Christ?

That those whom God the Father gave to his Son to redeem (John 17:6—"thine they were and thou gavest them me") were "purchased" is liberally stated on the pages of the New Testament. At Ephesians 1:7 it is said that "We have redemption through his blood," and the Greek word that is translated there as "redemption," ἀπολύτρωσιν, *apolutrōsin*, carries the clear meaning of "buying back" or "by paying of a ransom."[7] The underlying Greek word λύτρον, *lutron*, along with its cognates such as the verb form λυτρόω, *lutroō*, means the "price of release, ransom" or again, "making free by paying a ransom."[8] The apostle Paul has emphasized the same reality when he cautions the Corinthian church: "Ye are not your own; for ye are bought with a price," (1 Cor 6:19–20, 7:23). And in direct language our Lord himself said that he came "to give his life a *ransom* [λύτρον, *lutron*] for many" (Matt 20:28; Mark 10:45).

What has just been said contributes to the larger context in which our text at Acts 20:28, stating that Christ "purchased the church," is to be read. The New Testament pages are redolent with that statement of fact. But further light is thrown on the matter by reference to God's relation to his church, as that was expressed in its Old Testament form. In writing Acts 20:28, Paul may well have adapted the language of Psalm 74:2, where the notion of purchase is clearly in view: "Remember thy congregation, which

2. Berry, *Greek New Testament*.
3. Brown and Comfort, *Greek-English New Testament*.
4. Marshall, *Greek-English New Testament*.
5. Van der Pool, *The Apostolic Bible Polyglot*.
6. Bauer et al., *Greek-English Lexicon*, 655.
7. Ibid., 95.
8. Ibid., 483–84.

## The Divine Purchase

thou hast purchased of old."[9] If Paul at Acts 20:28 in any sense recalled Psalm 74:2, he has adapted the word "congregation," in the Septuagint (the Greek translation of the Hebrew Old Testament that was produced in the second century before the birth of Christ) to the word "church." But again, the concept of ransom is clear in Psalm 74:2, where the verb in the Septuagint, meaning "to ransom," is used. In the same connection we may reflect on God's promise in Hosea 13:14, where God says that he will *ransom* his people. The Septuagint at that point employs the word λυτρώσομαι, *lutrōsomai*, which, as we have seen, conveys precisely the fact of ransom.

At issue in the preceding comments is the fact that the larger context, not only of the New Testament Pauline literature, but also of the anticipatory Old Testament revelation, contributes to the interpretation and translation of the New Testament Greek. That larger contextual translation suggests quite firmly that Acts 20:28 is to be read as stating that God *purchased* the church. That, in turn, lies behind and justifies the statement of the *Westminster Confession* that Christ *purchased* for believers certain freedoms that now engage us.[10] The authors of our confessional standards planted their feet on firm doctrinal ground.

If, then, we hold that Christ *purchased* the church and that he actually paid the price of redemption and did not in some not-clearly-stated way merely *obtain* the church, the question follows as to what was the price that was paid for the ransom in view. Again the answer is copious in the New Testament literature. It was Christ himself who "*his own self* bore our sins in his own body on the tree" (1 Pet 2:24). It was Christ "who through the eternal Spirit *offered himself* without spot to God" (Heb 9:14) to "purge our sins" (Heb 1:3). The letter to the Hebrews rehearses at length the fact that Christ was the priest who made the definitive offering for sin, and that in doing so he was himself the sacrifice. Christ gave himself for our redemption.

Recalling now our discussion in the preceding chapter of the personhood of Christ, it was the *Person* of Christ himself who redeemed us by his substitutionary life and death. We say, that is, that it was the *divine Person* of Christ who died *in his human nature*. Paul's argument to the Corinthians has eloquently made the point. For as to the identity of Christ, "None of the princes of this world knew; for had they known it, they would not have

---

9. My attention to the citation of Psalm 74 has been drawn by Knowling in his *The Acts* in Nicoll, 2:436–37.

10. Recall that the same statements are contained in the (Congregational) *Savoy Declaration of Faith* and the (Baptist) *Second London Confession*.

## The Divine Purchase

crucified the Lord of glory" (1 Cor 2:8). It was the Lord of glory who died for us. And that reality, of course, enabled Paul to state in Acts 20:28 that it was "God [who] purchased the church with his own blood."

When it is said that it was the *Person* of Christ who discharged to the full his messianic assignment, it is clear that the divine nature of our Lord was engaged, along with his human nature, in his messianic accomplishment. There was, of course, a communication between the divine and the human minds (without, as has been said, a communication of properties) of our Lord, and he was at the same time supported in all that he did by the Holy Spirit who had been given to him "without measure" (John 3:34). Indeed, all that Christ did in this world he did in the strength of the Holy Spirit. We have it in Hebrews 9:14 that it was "through the eternal Spirit" that he "offered himself without spot to God." In the history of commentary a difference of view has been held as to whether the reference to the Spirit in that text is to be taken to refer to our Lord's divine nature or to the Person of the Holy Spirit. I suggest the latter. An expansive discussion on the point is contained in John Owen's exposition of the letter to the Hebrews.[11]

In earlier contexts we have inspected the fact that in accordance with the divine intention our first parent, Adam, was constituted as the federal head, or the representative head, of the race. When we looked at the fact and the meaning of his fall into sin we saw that "all mankind, descending from him by ordinary generation [thus excepting the Lord Jesus Christ who was born of the virgin], sinned in him and fell with him in his first transgression."[12] The fact is that, as a consequence of our relation to Adam, the guilt of his sin was imputed to us, or, that is, was placed to our account. In the initial created state we were *in Adam*, and as such shared the responsibility for what Adam did. If, in his probation, he had obeyed and kept the law that God had communicated to him, we would have shared in his promised elevation to eternal life. Of course, Adam did not sustain his probation and it is to a degree speculative as to what would have been the result of obedience. But at least the following can be said. The first Adam, we have it at Romans 5:14, was a type of the second (see 1 Cor 15:45, 47). We shall refer in a moment to what it was that the second Adam, Jesus Christ, came into the world to do. But because the second Adam was rewarded for *his* obedience, and on the ground that he was the antitype of the first Adam, it is consequential to say that Adam would have been

---

11. See Owen, *Hebrews*, 6:303–307. See also Owen, *Works*, 3:168, 176.
12. Westminster Shorter Catechism, Question 16.

rewarded for *his* obedience. In the outcome, we have shared in the malediction, rather than benediction, that Adam suffered by reason of his fall. At the fall, we were constituted sinners and we therefore come into the world as sinners with a fallen nature. The imputation of Adam's guilt to all his natural posterity, moreover, was an immediate imputation. The statement that it was *immediate* and not *mediate*, means that there was no mediating thing or entity on the grounds of which we were considered guilty because of Adam's sin. The use of the word *immediate* in that context does not refer to immediacy in time. It is true that, in the temporal sense, the guilt was placed to our account immediately after our first parent fell. But what is involved in the imputation of sin is that it occurred simply, directly, and on the grounds that God, in his act of creation, had placed the entire human race in a relation of solidarity with Adam. There can be no point in raising the question of why that should have been the divine plan and intention at the point of creation. It is beyond our prerogative and capacity to inspect to its full extent, or to argue against, the dictates of the eternally sovereign will and purpose of God. The fact is as it is in the revelation that God has made.

The apostle has stated the case in clear terms in his letter to the Romans. "By one man [Adam] sin entered into the world, and death by sin; and so death passed upon all men" (Rom 5:12). And "in Adam all die" (1 Cor 15:22). But Paul, in that highly significant paragraph in his letter to the Romans, crystallizes also the salvific implications of the person and work of Christ. The nub of the argument there is that, as Adam was the federal head of the race that was to come from him, so Christ is the federal head of those whom he has redeemed. The federal headship of Christ stands determinatively against that of Adam. Paul drives home the point. "If through the offence of one many be dead, much more the grace of God, and the gift of grace . . . hath abounded unto many" (Rom 5:15). "If by one man's offence death reigned by one; much more they which receive abundance of grace and the gift of righteousness shall reign in life by one, Jesus Christ" (Rom 5:17).

The outcome turned on the matter of obedience to God's holy law. We have observed that the initial covenant with Adam contained within its terms certain promises of blessing and benediction in the event of Adam's obedience, and promises of curse and malediction in response to disobedience. The obligations upon which the promises were suspended were conveyed clearly to our first parent. Now that Christ came into the world to assume substitutionary responsibility for the people for whom he gave his life, he assumed the obligations of God's covenants on their behalf. "He became obedient unto death" (Phil 2:8). Paul clinches the case: "As by one man's disobedience many were made sinners, so by the obedience of one shall many be made righteous" (Rom, 5:19). That being so, the obedience that Christ offered includes what has been referred to as his active obedience and his passive obedience. We encountered the terms in earlier contexts. Christ was our substitute in both those respects. His active obedience was his keeping the law of God perfectly on our behalf, and as a result of the imputation to us of the righteousness implicit in that obedience, God now looks on us as though we ourselves had kept the law. Christ's passive obedience was his dying to satisfy the penalty of the guilt of our sin on our behalf. Again, God now therefore looks on us as though we ourselves had paid the penalty for our sin.

There was, of course, a passive aspect in our Lord's active obedience, in that he voluntarily and purposefully submitted himself to the will of the Father. "I came down from heaven," he said, "not to do mine own will, but the will of him that sent me" (John 6:38). And in the darkness of that Gethsemane night he prayed, "nevertheless not as I will, but as thou wilt. . . . thy will be done" (Matt 26:39, 42). And there was an active aspect of our Lord's passive obedience. He voluntarily and purposefully laid down his life. In his discourse on his identity as the good shepherd who gives his life for his sheep, he stated that "No man taketh it from me, but I lay it down of myself" (John 10:18). Christ's passive obedience in submitting himself to the death of the cross may be understood as his final act of active obedience, for the law had said that "The soul that sinneth, it shall die" (Ezek 18:4). And it was precisely in obedient recognition and fulfillment of that law that Christ died for his people.

What amazing love, what remarkable condescension that the eternal Son of God should submit himself to the will of the Father to that complete extent. As to his eternal, ontological state of being he was one with the Father and the Holy Spirit. The full essence of the Godhead resides fully in each of the triune Persons. In what theologians have referred to as the ontological trinity, or the divine trinity considered in its ontological aspect (its aspect of being) there was no subordination. But as to the performance of the redemptive offices to which the Persons of the Godhead committed themselves in the determinate council before the foundation of the world, there was, as we have seen, a subordination of the Son of God to the Father. That relationship is referred to as an aspect of the economic trinity, or the divine trinity considered in its economic aspect. The word "economic" in

## The Divine Purchase

that statement refers to the distribution of redemptive offices to the distinguishable Persons of the Godhead.

But what is to be said as to the disposition of the price of redemption that was paid? If, as has been argued, a ransom was paid, to whom was it paid? It is not necessary to refer at any length to the fatuous suggestion that the ransom price was paid to the devil. The simple but profound reality is that the price was paid in satisfaction of the wrath of God against sin. That is precisely what is involved in the statement in the first epistle of John that "God loved us and sent his Son to be the propitiation for our sins" (1 John 4:10. See also Romans 3:25, Hebrews 2:17, and 1 John 2:2). Again there has been some divergence among theologians as to the translation of those texts. Some have preferred to translate the underlying Greek at 1 John 4:10, ἱλασμὸν, *hilasmon*, to state that Christ was the "expiation" for our sins. The word "propitiation" refers explicitly to setting at peace, in the case in hand the setting at peace of the wrath of God. "Expiation," on the other hand, refers to the erasure of guilt. And of course, Christ was both the expiation and the propitiation for our sin. But textual analysis supports the doctrine of propitiation at the point stated.[13] It is for that reason that Paul could say to the Romans that "Being justified by faith, we have peace with God" (Rom 5:1). At issue in that text is the fact that God is now at peace with his people. The demands of his holy justice have been completely satisfied.

What are we to say, then, of the transaction between the Father and the Son when, on the cross, Christ completed the purchase of our redemption? We recall that our Lord, while, as we have said, it was the Lord of glory who died, actually died for us *in his human nature*. But we hold in view at that point that our Lord was in possession of the full capacities of human nature, in soul and body. We hold, therefore, in holy reverence before the mystery that is involved, that in his dying Christ suffered in human soul and human body. In the agony of soul that he suffered he passed through eternal death on our behalf. He suffered the very pains of hell for us. On the cross he descended into hell. But he passed triumphantly through that eternal death and emerged victoriously. At that point Satan knew he had been definitively defeated. He saw and knew that those whom he might have attempted to destroy had been definitively rescued by Christ from his possible grasp. They now belonged to Christ. They were forever beyond the devil's grasp. He

---

13. See the extended discussion on the point in Morris, *Apostolic Preaching of the Cross*, 125–85.

might henceforth disturb their peace, and harass, and to a degree confuse them for a time. But now they were eternally secure in Christ.

Now that our Lord had passed triumphantly through eternal death he could lay down his human life in his temporal death. He was qualified to do the latter because of his triumph in the former. In due time he would commit his human soul to the Father. When he had said "It is finished" (John 19:30), reflecting what he had prayed in his high priestly prayer, "I have finished the work which thou gavest me to do" (John 17:4), he could say "Into thy hands I commend my [human] spirit" (Luke 23:46). He committed his human soul to the Father. It is clear, then, that the reference to the shedding of blood, as that encapsulated the accomplishment of redemption, is in a significant sense a synecdochical statement that brings to awareness the fact that the redemptive act of Christ involved a suffering of soul as well as of body. In that connection John Owen, referring to the meaning of the sacrifice that Christ offered as "a matter of great importance" to the extent of involving the suffering in his full human nature, has commented judiciously: "Those who look only *on the outward part* of the death of Christ can see nothing but suffering in it."[14] More was involved than the suffering perceived by those who look "only on the outward part." Owen goes on at length to consider the fact that "the principal consideration of it is his [Christ's] own offering of himself a sacrifice unto God, as the great high priest of the church, to make atonement and reconciliation for sinners, *which was hid from the world by those outward acts of violence which were upon him*."[15]

But why, we must ask further, does the Christian believer stand fully justified and the beneficiary of all of the saving graces of God as a result of the substitutionary atonement that Christ has made? The Scriptures are extensive in their display of the fact that there could be no salvation, no reconciliation with God, on the grounds of any work that we could do. It is by the grace of God that any are saved. "By grace are ye saved through faith; and that not of yourselves; it is the gift of God" (Eph 2:8). Christ himself is the object of our faith. But now the action of God the Father is involved in the outcome, in the application to the believer of the redemption that Christ accomplished. The outcome turns on what was anticipated in our reference to the substitutionary nature of all that Christ did for us (see Isa 53:4–5). That is, at the atonement of Christ there occurred what

---

14. Owen, "A Discourse concerning the Holy Spirit" in Owen, *Works*, 3:176, italics added.

15. Idem, italics added.

theologians have called a great exchange,[16] that takes up what is now to be recognized as a double, or reciprocal imputation.

As the sinner has been called and turned to Christ by the sovereign work of the Holy Spirit in the soul (which we shall return to more fully in the following chapter), on his repentance and faith in Christ, two levels of imputation occur. First, the guilt of the sinner's sin is imputed to Christ, or, that is, placed to Christ's account. We ask the question, then: Was Christ guilty when he died on the cross? The answer is yes, he was guilty, not of his own sin, because he was sinless, but of our sin that had been imputed to him. What, in other words, was the ground on which the Father could lay the burden of his wrath against sin on his own Son in the dark hours of the cross? God the Father who is holy and just in all his actions and deliberations could not in truth declare his Son to be guilty unless he was in fact guilty. In order, therefore, for God to truthfully *declare* his Son guilty, his Son, as a result of an action of the Father, must be *constituted* guilty. Precisely that state was brought to effect by the fact that the Father imputed to Christ the guilt of our sin. By that act of imputation, God the Son now truly guilty of our sin could bear the penalty of God's wrath against sin. But the guilt that Christ bore was our guilt. It was not, for him, an *intrinsic* guilt, for he was sinless. It was an *extrinsic* guilt. All that has been said implies that in that divine act of imputation Christ was constituted guilty, but he was not constituted a sinner.

But by reciprocity, the righteousness of Christ was imputed to the Christian believer. When the repentant sinner knelt at the cross of Christ he was, in every respect that was relevant to his status, ungodly. He was *ungodly* because he had not kept and obeyed the law of God. But now, as a result of the transactions that occurred, he was accounted *godly* in the accounts of heaven. He was now accounted just, or righteous, deemed to have kept the law. Again we should see that God who is just and righteous could not declare the sinner to be righteous unless he was in fact truly righteous. The eternal God of truth cannot lie. God must therefore take action to *constitute* the sinner righteous in order to be able to *declare* him righteous. That he does by imputing to him, or placing to his account, the righteousness of Christ.[17]

Again, it is clear from the scriptural data that the righteousness that is in that way imputed to the sinner is the *forensic* righteousness of Christ.

---

16. The relevant theological literature is copious. See Eveson, *The Great Exchange*.

17. The important issue of the imputation involved in the atonement that Christ offered is discussed definitively in Murray, *Romans*, 178–210.

## The Divine Purchase

"Forensic" means "in relation to law." And the righteousness of Christ that is imputed to the confessing believer is the righteousness that accrued to him by reason of his perfect keeping of the law. When we speak, then, of the reciprocal imputation that seals the Christian believer's status in the sight of God, two things are to be kept clearly in mind. First, it is not the sinner's *intrinsic sinful state* that is imputed to Christ. By that we mean that Christ himself does not become a sinner. He is not, as some theologies have said, *constituted* a sinner. Second, having said that by imputation the sinner receives the *forensic* righteousness of Christ, he does not acquire the *essential* holiness or righteousness of Christ that belongs to him by reason of his eternal possession of the full essence of the Godhead. The entrance to the kingdom of God does not involve the divinization of man.

Thus it is that, by the substitutionary life and work of Christ in this world, those that are brought by the Spirit of God to saving faith in Christ (John 6:44) have an indisputable and ineradicable title to heaven. Well might the apostle exclaim: "Thanks be unto God for his unspeakable gift" (2 Cor 9:15).

CHAPTER 6

# Partakers of Redemption

THE THEOLOGY DEVELOPED IN the Reformation century, by such Reformers among others as Calvin in Geneva, Bucer in Strasbourg, and Zwingli and Bullinger at Zurich, came to a high level of consolidation in the seventeenth century that followed. The most enduring English language Confession at that time, in a century that could properly say of its theologians that "There were giants in the earth in those days," was the *Westminster Confession of Faith* (1647), with its Shorter and Larger Catechisms. The larger compass of its theological developments and insights warrants the closest inspection. It throws unparalleled light on the questions we have raised.

What is to be said, we asked at the beginning, of the state and condition of human personhood? We answered the philosophers and the poets in their challenge to "know thyself," as it has been argued from the classic Greek philosophers onwards, by adducing the story of man as the Scriptures have declared it. It is not a story of a gradual ascent from whatever might have begun the journey, whether it was from the primeval mud and slime, or from a metamorphosis that at a point in time endowed a nonhuman entity with humanness and human impulses and capacities. The optimism of a century ago, that was all too quickly shattered by the twentieth century's wars and economic depression and cultural collapses, has faded. There is a jadedness about our affairs now, a seediness and a despair of discovering who man really is. Darwinism is no longer sure of itself. The brave anticipations of the evolutionists have been shattered by the sheer history of the world they mistakenly assumed was within their grasp. The collapse of earlier assumptions of the explanatory competence of reason has been followed by a pointless existentialism and even, in more recent times, by a postmodernism that admits that no final, unarguable, and sustainable explanation of anything exists anywhere. It is no longer possible, it is now argued, to think or to contemplate reality in terms of absolute propositions or claims to truth. Every man's truth is as good as every other man's truth. Conversation is relatively inconsequential, partial, relative, and without the benefit of absolute criteria of knowing and behavior. All is what it is, it is being said, as the outcome of a conjunction of random forces that it is impossible to corral completely in thought. Chance is king, and man himself is nothing but a chance phenomenon. He is therefore without explanation of himself, without explanation of why whatever exists is as it is.

The story of man is not, then, one of inevitable improvement, of cultural, social, and economic advance to an autonomously conjured terminus of bliss. Nor can it properly be said, as we observed at the beginning, that the attempt to travel well is more important, if satisfaction is to be found anywhere, than to arrive. The story of man, rather, is a story of a creation, in time that was created as the mode of his existence, of a person made in the image of God, in a state of unimaginable bliss but followed by a catastrophic fall. The state of human personhood is what it is because of the inheritance, by all people everywhere and at all times, of the entailment of our first parent's sin. We have looked at aspects of the case. But now a number of questions arise in the light of the fact that God, in the initiative and grace of his own will, set forth a way of reconciliation with himself. He sent his own Son into the world to be the redeemer of those whom, in the counsels of eternity, he chose to make up his eternal kingdom with him.

We saw in the preceding chapter that the Son of God came into the world that he might "purchase the church with his own blood" (Acts 20:28). The question arises, then, as to how sinful man is to experience, to take hold of, to be the beneficiary of, the redemption that has thereby been so lavishly provided. If, as has been argued, man in his natural state as he exists in this world is the slave of Satan and sin (Rom 6:16; John 8:44), if "The god of this world has blinded the mind" (2 Cor 4:4), if "The carnal mind is enmity against God; for it is not subject to the law of God, neither indeed can be" (Rom 8:7), and if the Scripture is true when it says that "The natural man receiveth not the things of the Spirit of God; for they are foolishness unto him; neither can he know them, because they are spiritually discerned" (1 Cor 2 :14)—if those things are true and if, as a result, man by nature is locked in a parlous condition of inability to know God, how, then, can he be the beneficiary of the grace of reconciliation that God has provided? It is precisely at that point that the glory of the gospel appears. Man can know God because God makes himself known.

## The Divine Purchase

Christ put the matter clearly and forthrightly in his remonstration with the Jews following his discourse on his identity as the bread of life. "No man can come unto me," he said, "except the Father which hath sent me draw him" (John 6:44). It is the fact that God the Father performs a sovereign, drawing work in the soul of a man that any person can and does turn in saving faith to Christ. Of those whom the Father draws to himself he said long ago, "I have loved thee with an everlasting love; therefore with lovingkindness have I drawn thee" (Jer 31:3). And Christ himself has therefore said: "All that the Father giveth me shall come to me; and him that cometh to me I will in no wise cast out" (John 6:37). In ways we have now to address, those whom God draws to himself he makes willing to come with a new freedom born of his gracious ministry to them. "Thy people shall be willing in the day of thy power" (Ps 110:3). Let us see briefly what is involved.

The Westminster Shorter Catechism asks our questions in the following manner: "How are we made partakers of the redemption purchased by Christ?" and the answer follows: "We are made partakers of the redemption purchased by Christ, by the effectual application of it to us by his Holy Spirit."[1] Coming into focus at that point is what we have already referred to as the redemptive office of the Holy Spirit. We recall that at the council of redemption before the foundation of the world, when the distinguishable Persons of the Godhead undertook certain redemptive offices, it was the voluntarily assumed office of the Holy Spirit, the blessed Third Person of the divine Trinity, to call to Christ those for whom he died and to apply to them the gifts and benefits that Christ purchased for them. How, then, does an individual, locked and lost in sin, come to faith in Christ to the eternal salvation of his soul? The answer, we are beginning to see, is that by the work of his Holy Spirit and as an action of his grace, God draws the sinner to himself in Christ.

But how is that "drawing" of God's grace to come to effect? The Catechism continues: "The Spirit applieth to us the redemption purchased by Christ by working faith in us, and thereby uniting us to Christ, in our effectual calling."[2] We recall that in his nocturnal encounter with Nicodemus, our Lord had marveled at Nicodemus's inability to grasp what was being said to him, and he put the issue bluntly, "Except a man be born again, he cannot see the kingdom of God" (John 3:3). Nothing less radical must occur as affecting the entire personhood of the individual than what is here called

---

1. Westminster Shorter Catechism, Question 29.
2. Ibid., Question 30.

a new birth. The Spirit of God takes hold of a man and performs such a work of renewal within the soul, by applying to him the benefits that Christ purchased for him, that the only way to describe the outcome is as the apostle states it: "If any man be in Christ, he is a new creature; old things are passed away; all things are become new" (2 Cor 5:17). The man is simply not what he was before. Something has happened to him that makes it possible to say that he is a new person. Something, that is, has happened within the very essentials of what establishes his personhood that makes him simply a new man. We must not diminish the magnitude of what is involved.

The apostle has encapsulated the outcome of that radical work of the Spirit of God in the soul by stating that God "hath delivered us from the power of darkness, and hath translated us into the kingdom if his dear Son" (Col 1:13). That is what occurs. There has been a complete transference from one kingdom to another. Once the man was the careless, somnolent slave of the devil, kept in calm unconcern by the "strong man armed," the devil to whom our Lord referred in Luke 11:21. Now he has been joined to Christ in a completely new and different kingdom. The apostle John in his first epistle makes the similar observation that those whom the Spirit of God takes hold of in those ways are now people who are "walking in the light" (1 John 1:7). There are just two kinds of people in the world, John is saying. There are those who "walk in the light" of fellowship with God, and there are those who still "walk in darkness" (1 John 1:5–7).

But the questions press. What, more precisely, is the nature of the work that the Spirit of God effects that results in such a radical change in individual personhood? What is it that we observed the Catechism to refer to as "effectual calling," whereby an individual is turned to Christ? The Catechism summarizes as follows: "Effectual calling is the work of God's Spirit, whereby convincing us of our sin and misery, enlightening our minds in the knowledge of Christ, and renewing our wills, he doth persuade and enable us to embrace Jesus Christ, freely offered to us in the gospel."[3] That, in short, is what our Lord referred to as the new birth that was necessary before any understanding of the things of God could be grasped, and before entrance to the kingdom of Christ could follow.

In more modern expressions, what has been referred to here as the individual's "effectual calling" is properly addressed under the heading of regeneration. The person whom God has made regenerate knows and understands and reacts positively to the overtures of God's grace. It might

---

3. Ibid., Question 31.

properly be said that what the Catechism has defined as effectual calling is wider in its intended compass than regeneration. For effectual calling as defined encompasses the broad arc of what happens to the individual from the initial impact of the Spirit's influence on the soul, up to the individual's actual "embrace of Jesus Christ." Regeneration may be understood as the sovereign work of the Holy Spirit that is defined within the larger view that is referred to as effectual calling.

In any event, in the definition as given it is highly significant that in some sense that can be defined or described further, what is involved is the work of the Spirit on and within the faculties of the soul. We have observed that in our father Adam's initial state there existed a harmony of the faculties, the intellectual faculty or the mind, the affective faculty or the emotions, and the volitional faculty or the will. With the mind Adam naturally knew God, with the affections he naturally loved God, and with the will he naturally obeyed God. The drastic result of the fall was that the harmony of the faculties was shattered, and the mind surrendered its hegemony to the affections, the lusts and the passions. But now, from the statement of the effects of effectual calling, each of the faculties is affected and renewed. In the definition as given we note that first, the faculty of intellect or mind is affected: "enlightening the mind in the knowledge of Christ"; the affections are engaged and the conviction of sin and misery results: "convincing us of our sin and misery"; and the volition or the action of the will is involved, in that the individual is now both persuaded and enabled to embrace Jesus Christ.

We may give an alternative statement of what is involved in this radical work of the Spirit of God in the soul that we are now referring to as regeneration. Regeneration, we may say, is that *secret, sovereign, and unsolicited* work of the Holy Spirit of God in the soul, whereby the faculties of soul are endowed with abilities and capacities they did not previously possess, and a new disposition or principle of action is implanted in the soul.

Regeneration is a "secret" work of the Spirit of God because of the fact that, apart from God's intervention, the soul is completely without any ability to turn to God. It is a secret work because it takes place in the subconscious level of the individual's personhood, and the individual himself has no part in it at all. The individual can have no part in his regeneration because, as has been adequately said, he is the slave of sin, the dupe of the devil. He has of himself, and he can have, no conception of the things that have to do with God and his effectual calling unless the Spirit of God intervene and enlighten him. Regeneration is a "sovereign" work of the Holy

Spirit because he does all things according to his sovereign will. There is no more ultimate explanation or cause of any thing or event in the world, we have said, than the will of God. He "worketh all things after the counsel of his own will" (Eph 1:11). The mind of God, the purposes of his will in their full explication, are beyond our capacity of comprehension. Are there mysteries, then, in the matter of God's declarations of purpose, and in the levels of comprehension with which we contemplate them? Of course. But in the presence of mystery the new-born child of God bows in worship, wonder, and praise.

We have said also that regeneration is an unsolicited work of the Spirit of God in the soul. No man becomes regenerate because he has asked God to make him regenerate. The thing is impossible, because until he is first the beneficiary of the enlightening and calling work of the Spirit of God he cannot possibly wish to have anything to do with God. In an important sense, then, every person who is made regenerate, born again and made a new creature as the apostle stated the case in 2 Corinthians 5:17 (cited above), is made the regenerate child of God in spite of himself. That statement, of course, should not be misunderstood. For it is true that as a result of the Holy Spirit's endowment of the faculties with new abilities and capacities, the individual whom the Spirit is drawing to Christ comes willingly and freely.

By virtue of his regeneration, the individual now sees and understands things that were previously completely foreign to him. His mind was previously darkened to them. He had no interest in them. They were, as Paul said to the Corinthians "foolishness unto him" (1 Cor 2:14). He may have heard the gospel a thousand times without any cognizance of its real terms at all. But now he hears the gospel, as it were, for the first time. It is now light before eyes that were previously blinded by Satan and sin. Now he sees and understands what the revelation of God had been saying to him all along. He now knows that the word of God is true, that his real position is as the word of God states it to be, that he is on the course to eternal perdition, but that God has made a way of reconciliation with himself. Now he sees, by reason of the gifts of repentance and saving faith, that the regenerating work of God has implanted in the soul, that he is free to turn to Christ and to know the joys of life everlasting.

Not only, in those ways, is the mind renewed with new capacities for vision. In regeneration the renewing work of the Spirit of God is effective in the emotional or affective faculty of the soul. If, as we have just said, the regenerate person now sees and understands with new insights of mind and with a new naturalness knows God for who he is, a God of grace, so in the same way he now, with a new naturalness, loves and seeks and reaches for the things of God. And again, the renewing work of the Spirit of God extends beyond the intellectual and the affective faculties to the volitional faculty, or the will. The regenerate person necessarily, freely, and willingly turns in confession of his sin to Christ. The Catechism we quoted put the case by stating that regeneration involved, first, the "convincing of sin and misery," the "enlightening of the mind in the knowledge of Christ," and "the renewing of the will." Now, therefore, the new-born person responds to the call of God with a new naturalness and freedom. It is with a renewed mind, a renewed heart, and a renewed will that an individual comes freely and uninhibitedly to Christ.

But that clear biblical doctrine has not always been the property of the church. And at the present time the doctrinal claims of the evangelical church in these matters are very various. The differences that exist turn on varying claims regarding the meaning of the atonement for sin that Christ has made. A defective understanding of the human condition, and therefore of man's abilities of soul, traces to the claims of a man known as Pelagius who flourished in the fourth century. He was at that time engaged in a debate with Augustine, whose counterarguments influenced the church's restatement of the biblical doctrine of salvation in the Reformation century and down to the present day.

For Pelagius, the fall of our first parents did not do damage to the faculties of the human soul, and the capacities of will remained such that while men ought to do good and seek after God, they were perfectly free and able to do so. Augustine argued to the contrary. In short, Pelagius argued that man in his soulish capacities was perfectly healthy. Roman Catholic theology took up the Pelagian apparatus of thought and became semi-Pelagian. It argued that man was not perfectly healthy but was sick. His sickness was such that in order to turn to God he needed a certain divine assistance. Thus there emerged the Catholic doctrine of congruent grace. If man did what he was able to do he would merit the assistance of grace that was, then, congruent with human action. Reformed theology, to the complete contrary, saw not that man was perfectly healthy or that he was sick; it saw, on the grounds both of biblical data and observable human experience, that man, as to his state of soul, was dead. He was in drastic need, not of semi-Pelagian congruent grace, but of a thoroughgoing renewal, a recreation, a new birth, a radical change that struck to the deepest depths of human being and character. But the church at this time, not only in its liberal expression but in broad contemporary evangelicalism, has been trapped in the barren contours of semi-Pelagianism.

Involved, as a result, is the doctrine of the extent of the atonement that we considered in the preceding chapter. Christ died, it has been said, for those who, before the foundation of the world the Father gave to him to redeem. Contrary to that biblical statement that we have examined at some length, Pelagian systems of theology argue that Christ died for all men indiscriminately. That is to say, in his death on the cross Christ provided the necessary atonement for all men's sins. The upshot of that doctrine is that Christ having thereby done all that was necessary for men's salvation, whether any man, then, was saved, depended simply and entirely on whether, with the perfect freedom of the faculties of soul that he is deemed to possess, he accepts the offer of salvation that Christ makes to him. What is being said under such a doctrinal system is that Christ died to make salvation possible, but that in and by his death he did not really save anybody. That is then presenting us with what we can call a possibility theory of salvation. But we do not say that Christ died merely to make salvation possible. In his death Christ actually saved the people for whom he died.

The Pelagian error was reintroduced into the church in the early seventeenth century by a theologian named Arminius. It was again essentially a possibility theory of salvation, grounded in the doctrine of a universal or general or indiscriminate atonement. The Arminian error was decisively rejected by the Synod of Dort in 1618–1619. But the errors continued to trouble the church. The struggle of Augustine against Pelagius was repeated in essence in that between Calvin and Pighius at the Reformation, and it recurred at the time of the evangelical awakening of the eighteenth century when George Whitefield stood for the biblical truth against the Arminian John Wesley. It continues to be the substantial position of many parts of the evangelical church at the present time.

The issues we have discussed to this point under the heading of regenerate personhood have given rise again to differences of doctrinal persuasion in the church at large. Let us look from a different perspective at the meaning for individual regenerate personhood of the atonement that Christ offered for sin. We recall from the discussion in the preceding chapter that whereas Adam was established as the federal head of all those who descended from him by ordinary generation, Christ is the federal head of all those for whom he died. The respective federal headships of Adam and Christ are spelled out in that very important paragraph in the fifth chapter of Paul's letter to the Romans that runs from the twelfth to the twenty-first verse. "In Adam all die" (1 Cor 15:22), but in Christ all those for whom he died are made alive unto new and eternal life. In his extended argument to the Romans, Paul states that the subjects of Christ's work of redemption were so intimately united to him that "our old man is crucified with him" (Rom 6:6). The "old man," all that it was that identified the believer with Adam, the Adamic man, died when Christ died. "Reckon ye also yourselves to be dead indeed unto sin, but alive unto God through Jesus Christ our Lord" (Rom 6:11). The radical nature of the transactions that thus occurred at the death of Christ is such that the believer in Christ is freed from the domain of sin, from the realm that has anything to do with bondage to sin, and is transferred to the realm of justification and life. In short, the old man is dead.

But some theologians have argued that that is all very well; the old man is dead, they say, but the old nature of the individual remains. Some go so far as to say that when subsequently the Christian believer sins, it is not the new nature in the person that sins, but the old nature. To such a claim we rejoin that when the Christian sins it is the *person* who sins, and it is the person who is responsible and accountable for his sin. But reflection on what we have adduced as the meaning of regeneration, and invoking, for example, the statement at 2 Corinthians 5:17 that the person who is now "in Christ" is a new creation, the focus of our thought falls securely on the fact that the regenerate believer is simply, as the text says, a new man. "All things have become new." We have already argued the case. If the individual is now a new person in the respects we have discussed, he is completely new, and it must as surely be said, not that there is in the Christian both an old nature and a new nature, but that the individual is simply new in all the respects relevant to regenerate personhood. The nature describes the person. And the regenerate man is a new person in a new nature.

That new nature is like the nature of God who has called him. The apostle Peter says that the regenerate person is now a "partaker of the divine nature" (2 Pet 1:4). That does not mean, of course, that the Christian has become in some sense absorbed into the divine essence of God. Regeneration does not involve or imply the divinization of man. Peter is saying that the regenerate person is now like God but not identical with God. He is like God in that, by God's conveyance to him of the grace of regeneration, he is placed in possession of aspects or elements of the communicable attributes of God.

When, then, the Christian sins, he sins in his new nature. That is the terrible fact about sin. The gravity of sin is displayed in the fact that it is the person, now joined to Christ in indissoluble union, as we shall see, that sins in his new nature.

Further blessings and benefits accrue to those who, as the *Westminster Confession* described them, are "partakers of the redemption purchased by Christ." We shall refer to aspects of them in the following chapters. We might sum up the significance of regeneration by observing that at that point there comes to effect (i) union with Christ, (John 17:23; 1 John 5:19–20); (ii) the sealing of, or by, the Spirit (Eph 1:13, 4:30), and (iii) the baptism of the Spirit (1 Cor 12:13). We shall observe that at the point of regeneration there comes to effect also the individual's adoption, in an objective sense, as a son into the family of God.

We sum up at this point by underlining the fact that at regeneration the new-born individual is joined to Christ in an organic, vital, spiritual, and indissoluble union, in response to which, in the light of his newly-established recognition of the fact and its reality, he unites himself to Christ. That he does by the exercise of faith, the ability for which was created within him by the very act of regeneration.

CHAPTER 7

# The Cosmic Significance of Christ

The apostle Paul, in his memorable meeting with the elders of the Ephesian church, defended his ministry to them by his claim that "I have not shunned to declare unto you all the counsel of God" (Acts 20:27). And what a remarkably comprehensive ministry and declaration of the redemptive purposes of God he had given to the church in his several missionary journeys. What remarkable providences of God had ordered his life. Born an Israelite of the tribe of Benjamin, a Pharisee whose life-bent began by his persecuting the church, inheriting Roman citizenship to which he was to appeal in certain instances of improper arrest, a scholarly man of high intellect who was mastered by the grace of God, Paul gave to the church both the outstanding systematic theology in his letters to the Romans and the Galatians and his extensive guidance on the Christian life, and the administration and worship of the church. His doctrinal insights command our closest attention and reflection.

Paul spelled out his divinely conveyed commission when, in the course of his apologia before king Agrippa prior to his deportation to Rome, he reported his arrest by God on the road to Damascus: "I have appeared unto thee," Christ declared to him, "delivering thee from the people, and from the Gentiles, unto whom I now send thee, to open their eyes, and to turn them from darkness to light, and from the power of Satan unto God, that they may receive forgiveness of sins, and inheritance among them which are sanctified by faith that is in me" (Acts 26:16–18). It is by faith in the Christ who appeared to Paul at midday on the Damascus road that all the blessings of salvation come. In the commission he received, Paul was uniquely appointed as the apostle to the Gentiles.

The focus of our thought in these brief studies has been on Paul's remarkable statement to the Ephesian elders: "God purchased the church with his own blood" (Acts 20:28). The spread of the gospel from Jerusalem and Judea, through Samaria to the predominantly Gentile areas (Acts 1:8) is recorded extensively in the New Testament. It had been promised long ago: "Japheth shall dwell in the tents of Shem" (Gen 9:27). The history of the subsequent expansion of the church is recorded in an extensive literature that is worthy of our closest study. Christ had said that he would build his church and that the gates of hell would not prevail against it (Matt 16:18). The fuller story of that building and expansion cannot engage us in our present space. But it is neglected by the Christian only to his impoverishment. Let us take, rather, particular note of the beginning stage of that process, or, in other words, the point at which, in God's unfolding of the historical accomplishment of his redemptive purposes, the doors of the kingdom of God were thrown wide open to the Gentiles.

The work of Christ expands beyond his work of redemption in his fulfillment of the redemptive office he assumed in the eternal determinate council of the Godhead. We shall speak in a moment of what we refer to as the cosmic significance of Christ. By that we shall refer to the larger scope of Christ's discharge of his eternally conceived, and in due time implemented, offices. But it is abundantly clear from the Scriptural record that a paramount office of our Lord was discharged in the reconciliation of his church with God the Father that he effected in his incarnate state.

We saw previously, in our reference to the *Westminster Confession of Faith* that, in his redemptive work, Christ purchased for his people "freedom from the condemning wrath of God and from the curse of the moral law."[1] At issue in the freedom from the curse of the law is the establishment of the one church in which both the Jews and the Gentiles are included. That is contemplated in Paul's letter to the Ephesians where he says that, by reason of the redemptive work of Christ, God has "broken down the middle wall of partition" between the Jews and the Gentiles and has made "of twain one new man" (Eph 2:15). The Confession, in some editions of which proof texts are referenced, cites Galatians 3:13 in support at that point. It will be useful, therefore, to consider at least briefly at this stage what that text states and implies.

Again, it is necessary to bear in mind the need for a contextual exegesis of the paragraph in which that proof text is found. When it is said that "Christ hath redeemed us from the curse of the law, being made a curse for us" (Gal 3:13), the first question to be resolved is who is the "us" who,

---

1. *Westminster Confession of Faith*, XX:1.

in that context, are said to have been redeemed from the curse? To answer that question we note from Galatians 3:10 that "As many as are under the works of the law are under the curse." So that in view at that point is the relation between those who had been given the law and the curse that followed from a failure to fulfill the demands of that law. That in itself is simply a reproduction of the statement in Deuteronomy 27:26, where it is said: "Cursed be he that confirmeth not all the words of this law to do them." That statement contemplated the Mosaic Law as it had been given in its complete codified form. Now it follows from the Galatian paragraph that those, then, who were liable to curse for having failed to fulfill the law were those to whom the law had been given. They, of course, were the nation-church of Israel, those whom God had chosen as his separate people, a special people for a special purpose. It follows further that those to whom the law had not been given, the Gentile nations separate from Israel, could not have been subject to potential curse of that law because they were not exposed to its precepts in the same direct way as were the Israelites. If they had not been in possession of the law they could not have been subject to any curse for not having kept the law.

Before we answer our question as to the identity of the "us" in Galatians 3:13, let us note a comment from the nineteenth-century Scottish theologian, John Brown: "I believe the more ordinary method among orthodox interpreters has been to understand the statement in the text as referring directly to all the saved— as a general statement of the way of salvation, and equivalent to, 'Christ has delivered *us elect sinners*,' or, '*us believers*, from the punishment which the divine law denounces on us as sinners, by having sustained that punishment in our room.' This, no doubt, is a truth.... [But] it will appear plain that this is not the apostle's meaning."[2] Brown goes on to say that "The Gentile believers were, previously to their conversion, under sin and condemnation, as well as the Jewish believers; but not being subject to the Mosaic law, they could not be considered as exposed to *its* curse, and, of course, they could not be represented as redeemed from a curse to which they were never subject."[3] John Brown's classic commentary is worthy of fuller notice.

Our answer to the question of the "us" in Galatians 3:13, then, is that the word refers to Jewish believers, those who had come to faith in Christ. Clearly, Christ had been made a curse on their behalf. Before we address

2. Brown, *Galatians*, 129.
3. Ibid., 129–130.

further the state of the Gentiles, let us observe the reason stated in the Galatian context for that deliverance from the curse. The answer to that question is given immediately in the following verse. It was in order, it is said, "That the blessing of Abraham might come on the Gentiles through Jesus Christ" (Gal 3:14). The blessing of Abraham as stated there refers to the blessing of justification by faith, through believing in Christ. It is necessary to see, therefore, a relation in the ordained ordering of God's redemptive decree between, first, the redemption of the believing Jews and second, the admission of the Gentiles to the blessing of Abraham.

What is being said is that in the implementation of the redemptive decree of God, a time would come when God's special relation to his special people, the nation-church of Israel, would be terminated. At that time the doors of the kingdom would be thrown wide open to the Gentiles. The promise of long ago, that "Japeth shall dwell in the tents of Shem" (Gen 9:27) would then be fulfilled. Galatians chapter 3 provides us with precisely that. As has been said, at that point the doors of the kingdom were thrown wide open to the Gentiles and the one church comprised of both Jews and Gentiles came into being through, and as a result of, the redeeming work of Christ. The law, in its codified, institutionalized form, we have seen, was given to the nation-church of Israel, not to the Gentiles. At Galatians 3:24, Paul says, "The law was our schoolmaster to bring us unto Christ." Careful note is to be taken, of course, that a function of the law is to convict of sin and thereby point the sinner to Christ. Paul had said to the Romans that "By the law is the knowledge of sin" (Rom 3:20). And he confessed that "I had not known sin, but by the law . . . but when the commandment came, sin revived, and I died" (Rom 7:7–9). But the "schoolmaster" function of the law in the Galatian text may be seen to have a quite different significance. For the purpose of the law, as it was given to Israel, was to hedge them in and keep them pure from the grossness of sin into which the surrounding nations had fallen. In that hedging-in function, the law was to preserve God's special people until, and for the purpose that, Christ the redeemer should in due time come from them as had been promised. The text in Galatians 3 goes on to say that "After that faith is come, we are no longer under a schoolmaster" (Gal 3:25). By that it is meant that when Christ had come the schoolmaster function of the law had been fulfilled.

But the question follows: Were not the Gentiles under a curse because of their failure to obey and honor the law of God? Of course they were. And the death of Christ redeemed the believing Gentiles from the curse they sustained. But a careful reading of Galatians 3 makes it clear that the law that was relevant to the curse that the Gentiles sustained was not the Mosaic law of which Galatians 3 is eloquent. What, then, was the law involved for the Gentiles? Clearly, it was the law of God as it had been given to Adam at the beginning. From another perspective we may recall that the obligations under the covenant of works, the obligations that accrued from the creation ordinances that God had given to our first parents, were not abrogated or dissolved when Adam fell. The covenant of works continued, and like all creation ordinances, simply because they were creation ordinances, that covenant remained obligatory on all people everywhere and at all times. The glory of the gospel is that, as we observed at an earlier stage, Christ came into the world to do for us what we were obligated to do under the covenant of works but could not do for ourselves. So that both the believing Jews and the believing Gentiles were redeemed from the curse they respectively sustained. The promise of Ephesians 2:15 was now fulfilled. There was henceforth one church in which both Jews and Gentiles shared common privileges and benefits. Or it could now be said that the one church of God that had been extant from the beginning, including "the church in the wilderness" (Acts 7:38) in the earlier form of administration of the covenant of grace, had now been established in the form it had been prophesied to assume within the new administration of the covenant.

But what is to be said of the status of those who, in the respects we have stated, are now within the church of God, Jews or Gentiles, whatever their ethnic origin? The Jewish Christians are no longer subject to the Mosaic law in its ceremonial and civil aspects. And the Gentile Christians have seen the obligations under the covenant of works satisfied on their behalf. The Jews and the Gentiles are now brought together to acknowledge a common obligation under law. But in what sense is that so? While the Mosaic law in its ceremonial and civil aspects has been set aside and no longer provides criteria of behavior, the law in its moral aspect, or the moral law, continues to be the rule of life for the Christian.

What, then, is to be said in final response to the statement of the confession that we have addressed? There is a regal law that guides the Christian's life. It is the divine law of righteousness. And the recognition of it opens the way to the fullest examination of the Christian believer's responsibility for, and his progress in, growth in holiness and likeness to the image of Christ. Christ has sent his Holy Spirit to convey to Christian believers the gifts and benefits that Christ purchased for them, to conform them progressively to the pattern of holiness in Christ, and to conduct them at last to glory.

With the church established by virtue of the saving work of Christ in the world, we may reflect again, all too briefly, on the more expansive cosmic significance of Christ.[4] What is to be said on that level is in no sense to be separated, however, from the redemptive work of Christ. It is because of his faithful discharge of the redemptive necessities that were laid upon him that what is now about to be said has any meaning at all. Christ's life and death had precise salvific significance, as has now been seen at length. In his death he definitively saved his people. In his death he provided the necessary penal sacrifice for sin, in that he paid the penalty that was due by reason of the wrath of God against sin. But a wider and more comprehensive significance attaches to the redemptive work of Christ. The accomplishment of that work is too narrowly specified, and it is seriously diminished in its fuller import, if attention is paid only to its salvific effect. The Scriptures explain expansively that Christ paid the penalty for the sins of his people in his substitutionary death. He confirmed their title to heaven by his perfect keeping of the law of God in his active obedience.

But the significance of the Person and work of Christ has a wider and more comprehensive denotation. In his death he cleansed the universe from the effects of sin so that a new heaven and a new earth will be established "in the dispensation of the fullness of times" (Eph 1:10). He made possible his own reign and rule of authority at the right hand of the Father, and he will gather his redeemed people to his eternal reign with him (2 Tim 2:12). Those uncompromising motifs come to prominence under the heading of the cosmic significance of Christ.

Consider from that aspect the salvation and eternal security of those whom Christ redeemed. In the wider terms now in view they were, by reason of the intratrinitarian communication and assignment, always entrusted to his care. That is so in the respect, firstly, that Christ was the agent of their creation. As the apostle Paul explained, it was by Christ, "The image of the invisible God . . . [that] all things were created, that are in heaven, and that are in earth, visible and invisible . . . all things were created by him, and for him" (Col 1:15–16). But the meaning of that statement is not exhausted by the recognition that Christ was the agent of creation in accordance with the

---

4. The following paragraphs are dependent on my unpublished paper, "'Heir of all things,' The Cosmic Significance of Christ," presented to the conference of the New England Reformed Congregational Fellowship in April, 2005. They have also appeared in Vickers, *Divine Redemption*, 140–48.

will of the Father. As Paul has stated it, the entire creation was "*for* him" as well as "*by* him." That initial assignment of creation in real historical time, or more precisely *into* time, points to the end for which God created the world. In doing all that he has done, God the Father's objective was that the Son might be glorified. It was not only in relation to his earthly assignment that the Father could and did say of the Son that it is he "in whom I am well pleased" (Matt 3:17), or that he was referred to as "my beloved Son" (Luke 9:35). The intratrinitarian honor and mutual glorification existed eternally, before the beginning of time, and God's creation and redemptive designs proceeded in accordance with its terms and imperatives.

The biblical doctrine of the being of God requires it to be said that the Persons of the Godhead are characterized by distinguishable properties. It is the distinguishable property of the Father that he generated the Son from all eternity. It is the distinguishable property of the Son that he was generated from the Father. The Son is the only begotten son of the Father. That statement does not imply a divine subordination within the Godhead. The Son, and also the Holy Spirit who proceeded from the Father and the Son, are autotheotic.[5] They are fully God in their own right, as the Father is God. The three Persons of the Godhead being of one substance, and the full essence of the Godhead residing fully in each of the Persons, there is no subordination of Persons within the Godhead considered in its ontological aspect, or, that is, as to its own eternal being. It is proper to speak, of course, of an economic subordination of the Son to the Father, meaning by that subordination in the discharge of the assigned and undertaken office of Messiah-redeemer. In that office and capacity Christ came, he said, to do the will of the Father. But he said with equal necessity and import that "I and my Father are one" (John 10:30). There is no subordination of, or between, the Father, the Son, and the Holy Spirit, regarded and worshiped as the ontological trinity.

In the mutual glorification of the Father and the Son, the work of creation was entrusted to the Son in order that he might have in his care, at all times and in all respects, those whom he had already agreed to bring to glory. But the process of redemption to which Christ had committed himself is understood more comprehensively when account is taken of the time dimension in which that process is being worked out. In that time process, the cosmic significance of Christ, who exists in his eternal identity as God outside of time, is expressed in the preservation of the world in

---

5. Recall the Trinitarian statement by Berkhof in chapter 3 above.

order that those who were redeemed by Christ, including, notably, those still to be born, will come to him. That work of preservation in time is being effected by reason of God's sovereign providence and his eventuation of all of human history. And it is the Spirit of Christ, the Holy Spirit whom he has sent into the world from the Father, who is the agent of that preservation and operation.

In that respect the further, or second, implication of the cosmic significance of Christ comes to prominence. That, to put it briefly, is that the doctrine of God's common grace, by which he eventuates all that occurs, is to be considered under the heading of the significance of the work of Christ. Common grace falls under the rubric of Christology. The work of Christ spreads its influence in preserving the world and human history until the full number of "Abraham's seed" has been brought to the realization of their redemption by Christ. Christ is the determiner and preserver of culture. It is by reason of Christ's redemptive assignment that the common grace of God is effective to the achievement of its divinely conceived objectives.

It follows that the cosmic significance of Christ extends not only to the preservation of the world in a bare or indifferent sense. At issue also is the fact that Christ's interest in the preservation and salvation of his people extends to his positive determination of the entire history and development of human culture. That he effects by the operation of his common grace. God is thereby at work eventuating the whole of human history in the interests of his church. That is the larger extent to which Christ, not only by his assumption of human nature but now by his immanent involvement in human history, has subjected himself to the context and passing of historical time.

The third respect in which the cosmic significance of Christ is to be observed was stated by the apostle Paul in his letter to the Ephesians. His statement bears directly and forcibly on the Christian's eschatological hope. There is, Paul said there, a mystery in the will of God, aspects of which, however, have now been made clear (Eph 1:9). God has established a purpose which he is bringing to full consummation in and by Christ. God, Paul says, has now "made known unto us the mystery of his will, according to his good pleasure which he hath purposed in himself," and the description of that eschatological purpose follows: "That in the dispensation of the fullness of times he might gather together in one all things in Christ, both which are in heaven, and which are on earth, even in him" (Eph 1:9–10).

## The Divine Purchase

The cosmic significance of Christ, Paul is saying, extends beyond the salvation of his people in any singular or isolated sense. Two more expansive realities are involved. First, the salvation of his people is now to be seen as part of an extensive design whose objectives and implications extend to the re-creation and rehabilitation, the renewal and the eternal preservation, of all things. It is Christ who, by his work of redemption, has cleansed the universe of sin, makes possible God's ultimate establishment of the new heaven and the new earth. In and by him, as the Ephesian text has stated, all things will again be gathered together in one. At Ephesians 1:10 the Greek text uses one word which we have translated as "gather together in one." And that Greek word contains the prefix ανα, *ana*, which imports the sense, in the compound word in which it appears, of "again," or "by way of recapitulation." The statement being made is that in Christ all things will be gathered together "again." The implication is that all things were subject to disruption and decay by reason of Adam's fall. Not only was man himself subject to the disabilities, the deprivation, and depravation that sin introduced. A generalized and universal disruption and decay occurred. "The creature [creation] was made subject to vanity . . . [but] the creature [creation] itself also shall be delivered from the bondage of corruption [decay] . . . For we know that the whole creation groaneth" (Rom 8:20–22). The apostolic statement at that point is that all things will again be restored to their primeval harmony, goodness, and beauty, and that by reason of the work of Christ that glorious eschatological terminus will be realized.

The more expansive implications of Christ's redemptive work is that his redeemed people are now joined to him in an organic, vital, spiritual, and indissoluble union. They are thereby introduced to a union within a redeemed church that is Christ's property, in that it was given to him by the Father before the foundation of the world. It is in Christ that those who are redeemed by him are incorporated into the union of the church as indefectible members. He is head of the church he has redeemed. That establishes the organic dimension of our salvation. The organism into which they are introduced and indissolubly established is the church. The Scriptures are replete with statements to that effect. "Christ loved the church," the same letter to the Ephesians states, "and gave himself for it" (Eph 5:25). And it is the church that God in Christ has "purchased with his own blood" (Acts 20:28). Further, those realities establish the Christian's eschatological hope, in the respect that that hope is itself an organic expectation. The Christian has not only been redeemed as a personal and private entity, but he is being

## The Cosmic Significance of Christ

prepared for eternal participation in the prospective glorification of the church, into union with which he has been called.

A fourth aspect of the cosmic significance of Christ follows from his redemptive accomplishment. Christ came to be for the sinners he redeemed their substitute prophet, priest, and king. By reason of Adam's fall and his repudiation of his covenantal obligations we were constituted sinners (Rom 5:12); and by virtue of the imputation to us of the guilt of his sin, and the transmission to us of a fallen nature, we, like Adam, are disabled from fulfilling the demands of those initially mandated offices. Christ came to do for us what we were obligated to do but could not do for ourselves. But Christ now fulfills the office of king, as well as that of prophet and priest. That kingship is implicit in what has already been said regarding the rule and reign of Christ. He has been established by the Father in his position of authority in recognition of his faithful completion of his redemptive assignment. Christ rules as king, over the church that he has bought with his own blood, and over the entire reality, and the history of that reality, external to the Godhead that God spoke into existence.

A fifth aspect of the cosmic significance of Christ holds important significance for a Reformed theological apologetic. It rests in the fact that Christ has come into the world as the sinner's substitute prophet. Leaving aside a fuller discussion at this point, the essence of the prophetic office, as that was at first mandated to Adam, was that of investigating, understanding, and explaining back to God the meaning of the reality-environment in which our first parents came to self-consciousness and awareness. God gave to Adam at that time all necessary principles and categories of explanation and criteria of truth and validity. But those principles, categories, and criteria were lost in Adam's false assertion of autonomy and his fall. His false epistemological assertion was that he could find within himself, or within intramundane reality, or within a social context of opinion, all necessary principles of knowledge and criteria of truth and meaning. He did not need, he decided, the principles of interpretation that God had at first communicated to him. But Christ has again disclosed to his people the true principles of understanding and the predication of meaning. Those know truly who know God truly. All things belong to Christ. All things and all that eventuates in human history are what they are, and they eventuate in the manner and in the structures they do, because Christ thought them before the foundation of the world. Christ established the laws of their being and function. All things are interpretable for the Christian only as they are interpreted christologically. They have meaning only as they are interpreted as belonging to, and determined by, Christ.

The final aspect of cosmic significance returns us to the Colossian text we have cited. Christ is there said to have been the agent of creation of all things. All things were created "*by* him" and "*for* him." It was for the glory of Christ that all things have been brought into existence. All things not only exist and function now for his glory, but everything will minister to his glory in the ages to come. That, again, points to the reality that the end for which God ordained all things is that his Son might be glorified.

All that exists is what it is because Christ thought it before the foundation of the world. All things belong to him. He is before all things, and in all things he has the preeminence. Because all the facts of history are his facts, and because they cohere and function by his created laws of being and operation, all things, and every aspect of reality, are to be interpreted by reference to him and his redeeming grace.

That, finally, is the extent of the cosmic significance of Christ and of what he has done in obedience to the Father's will. Christ has been appointed by the Father "heir of all things" (Heb 1:2). And he has called his church to share that eternal inheritance with him.

CHAPTER 8

# The Christian's Benefit in Christ

IN LIGHT OF WHAT has been said regarding the human condition, the inherited state of sin, the inability to turn willingly to seek God in Christ that plagues the human condition, and the rescue that is provided only by God's drawing the sinner to himself (John 6:44; Jer 31:3), the conclusion follows that salvation is all of grace. Paul had stated the case to the Ephesian Christians: "By grace are ye saved through faith; and that not of yourselves; it is the gift of God" (Eph 2:8). Some difference of view has been held as to whether in that statement it is "faith" or the entire process of salvation that is the gift of God. In the end, of course, both interpretations come to the same thing. For faith, that is saving faith in the Lord Jesus Christ, lies at the heart of salvation's endowment. It is sufficient to say at that point that by the regenerating work of the Holy Spirit in the depths of the soul, the gifts of repentance and saving faith accrue to the sinner whom God draws to himself.

Saving faith is not, and cannot be, the self-determined action of an autonomous individual who imagines he possesses the ability of soul to turn to God at any time. Such a supposition, we have seen, lies at the heart of the false assessment of human personhood insisted on by Pelagius centuries ago. That false teaching, that has plagued the church by its repeated recrudescence over the years and which informs much of evangelical doctrine at the present time, bears recollection. Pelagius argued that an individual's faculties of soul were not in any respect changed or affected by Adam's fall. Man ought to obey God, he said, and if he chose to do so he could. That system of thought ignores what we have seen as the disabilities introduced to the faculties, the intellectual, affective, and volitional faculties, or the mind, the heart, and the will, by the bondage to sin that the fall implied. On the contrary, the free gift of faith, the grace of regeneration, the new birth by the power of God, is the necessary precondition of a person's coming to Christ and claiming the gift of salvation.

What, then, is to be said of the on-going endowments of grace that determine and give shape to the life of the new-born Christian person? What are the endowments and blessings on the one hand, and the obligations and responsibilities on the other, that devolve on the Christian believer? They can be variously stated. The blessings are summarized in the Westminster Shorter Catechism that we have cited previously: "They that are effectually called do in this life partake of justification, adoption, and sanctification, and the several benefits which in this life do either accompany or flow from them."[1] Justification is that declarative, forensic statement by God that the sinner, who is *ungodly* in his sight because he has not kept the law of God, is now stated to be *godly* because the righteousness of Christ had been imputed to him and placed to his account. "Sanctification is the work of God's free grace, whereby we are renewed in the whole man after the image of God, and are enabled more and more to die unto sin, and live unto righteousness."[2] More expansively, "The benefits which in this life do accompany or flow from justification, adoption, and sanctification, are, assurance of God's love, peace of conscience, joy in the Holy Ghost, increase of grace, and perseverance therein to the end."[3] We shall return below to the obligations that are correspondingly laid upon the Christian believer.

Anticipating what we are now addressing as the Christian's benefits in Christ, we observed at the end of chapter 6 that at the point of regeneration there comes to effect certain individual benefits: first, union with Christ, (John 17:23; 1 John 5:19–20); second, the sealing of, or by, the Spirit (Eph 1:13, 4:30); and third, the baptism of the Spirit (1 Cor 12:13).

The sealing of the Spirit refers to that sovereign act of God by his Spirit whereby his seal is placed upon those whom he draws to himself. The function of a seal, such as a seal placed on an important document, is to indicate and preserve ownership or possession of that item by the person implanting the seal. The seal is an indication of property rights. So it is with the fact that God places his seal on those who belong to him. God having by his Holy Spirit brought a sinner to himself, having performed within the soul of such a person his secret, sovereign, and unsolicited work of regeneration and thereby conveyed to him saving faith in Christ, the individual now

---

1. Westminster Shorter Catechism, Question 32.
2. Ibid., Question 35.
3. Ibid., Question 36.

partakes of the nature of God himself. We have looked at that important fact of God's working by his Spirit in the act of regeneration, and by saying that the regenerate person partakes of the nature of God it is not intended to say that he is in some sense assumed into the very essence of the Godhead. But he is now holy, set aside for God, transferred from the kingdom of darkness into the kingdom of God's dear Son.

The seal is God's seal. It identifies the person sealed as now belonging to God and the property of God who placed the seal. At Ephesians 1:13 Paul states that "Ye were sealed with that Holy Spirit of promise," or by the Holy Spirit who had been promised. In the same letter Paul argued that those who have thus been sealed as God's property must therefore walk in this world in such a way that they "grieve not the Holy Spirit of God, whereby ye are sealed unto the day of redemption" (Eph 4:30). Because those individuals now belong to God they exhibit the character of God, and God looks upon them and knows that they are his. He knows his own people. Christ had said the same thing when, in his discourse on his identity as the good shepherd who gives his life for his sheep, he said: "He calleth his own sheep by name" (John 10:3). When our Lord died on the cross he knew the very names of those for whom he died. He knew their names because he had written their names in the book of life before the foundation of the world (Rev 13:8, 17:8). What a remarkable fact of Christian being, to have been sealed by the gracious sovereign will of God as his own property.

That God thereby knows those who belong to him is underlined by the apostle in his letter to Timothy: "The foundation of God standeth sure, having this seal, The Lord knoweth them that are his" (2 Tim 2:19). That statement is in turn a reflection and confirmation of what God had said of his people in the earlier administration of his covenant of grace. In the Septuagint it is similarly said at Numbers 16:5 that "God knows the ones who are his."

We reflect also on the fact that the blessings conveyed at the point of regeneration include the baptism of the Spirit. The doctrine of the Holy Spirit, his Person and his work and the offices he performs, not only in the administration of God's eternal purposes in general, but in the lives of the individual Christian in particular, has become an unsettled question in the church in its various denominational expressions. But the operative statement at the present point is clear, as the apostle Paul has stated to the Corinthians: "By one Spirit are we all baptized into one body, whether we be Jews or Gentiles, whether we be bond or free; and have all been made to drink into one Spirit" (1 Cor 12:13). By that spiritual baptism the Christian believer is inaugurated into the church of which Christ is the head. The individual is joined to Christ, as will be observed more fully in a moment, and he is therefore joined in a unity of all the members of the church whom Christ has redeemed to himself.

The promise that Christ made to his disciples has been fulfilled, and its benefits have accrued to all those who have been united to Christ through the testimony of the disciples that has come down through the ages. In his final supper with his disciples on the night on which he was betrayed, Christ made it clear that it was necessary that he should leave them. Conscious of their natural human sadness he said to them: "I will pray the Father, and he shall give you another Comforter, that he may abide with you for ever" (John 14:16). But more than that, in words whose meaning could not yet be grasped by the disciples, Christ promised: "I will not leave you comfortless; I will come to you" (John 14:18). That promise was fulfilled when Christ came again to his people by the sending of his Holy Spirit on the Day of Pentecost. Our Lord had said, moreover, that "When he, the Spirit of truth, is come he will guide you into all truth . . . he shall receive of mine and show it unto you" (John 16:13–14). Clearly, those words and that promise were made explicitly to his disciples, but it is equally clear that their promise and import accrue to all believers. We recall that in his high priestly prayer to the Father Christ prayed explicitly: "Neither pray I for these [the disciples] alone, but for them also which shall believe on me through their word" (John 17:20). Because the Holy Spirit came to those of the early church who were assembled and waiting for the fulfillment of the promise on the Day of Pentecost, the same blessings follow through the course of history and become the property of all who believe.

But the signal blessing that follows from all that has been said is that the Christian believer, by virtue of the regenerating work of God's Spirit within him is, in all the ways we have noted, joined in union to Christ. That union is a principal benefit and bequest to the soul by virtue of the salvation wrought by Christ in the perfect redemption he accomplished. That work was in fulfillment of the divine purpose of salvation and it realized the objectives of the eternal covenant of redemption. The union, which results from the fact that God by his Spirit has drawn his people to himself in Christ (John 6:44), is an organic, vital, spiritual, and indissoluble union. It is an organic union because, as has just been seen, it joins the Christian believer into a union with Christ that exists within the organism of the

## The Christian's Benefit in Christ

church that Christ redeemed. The church is joined to him as the body is to the head, receiving from him all necessary life sustaining power and influence. It is a vital union because it is a living union. It is real. It is actual. The very sensitivities, the predilections and progress in life of the Christian, are determined by the relationship with Christ that the union connotes. That was why the apostle could confess: "I live; yet not I, but Christ liveth in me; and the life which I now live in the flesh I live by the faith of [in] the Son of God, who loved me, and gave himself for me" (Gal 2:20).

The union is a spiritual union because the agent of its being and identity is the Holy Spirit of God. He has established it at the bequest of Christ who has sent his Spirit to his church for that very reason and with the ends of his corresponding purposes in view. The apostle John exhibits the same conceptions when he addresses the privileges of the Christian by his references to the presence of the Holy Spirit in and with them. John had differentiated the Christians to whom he wrote from all others by saying that "Ye have an unction from the Holy One," and again "The anointing which ye have received of him abideth in you" (1 John 2:20, 27). That union with Christ by his Spirit, John is saying in context, protects the Christian against the false teachings that abound and which would divert him from the joys of the fellowship with God the Father to which he has been called and in which he has been established.

Particular care is necessary at this point in understanding the meaning of what John is saying. First, this "unction [or this anointing, as in verse 27] of [or by] the Holy Spirit" is not to be understood as in some sense a special visitation of the Holy Spirit to certain individuals at certain stages of their progress in the Christian life and for certain special purposes. That the Holy Spirit does discharge his redemptive office in ways such as that is true and beyond doubt. God does, at special times and for special purposes, pour out his Spirit on the church in a way that speaks to the largeness of his purpose for it. The times of revival in the history of the church speak clearly to the point. But that is not what John is talking about in this context. For he is saying that this "unction" is something that every Christian has. It is part of the endowment that makes the Christian a Christian. It is a part of the essential conveyance to the Christian of the grace of God that establishes him in the fellowship with the Father of which John speaks consistently, and without which the individual is not living "in the light" but is still "in the darkness" (1 John 1:5–7). For John is quite explicit in saying that it is precisely this "unction" of the Spirit that makes it possible to say that the person who is the beneficiary of it "knows all things." That does not mean, of course, that the Christian knows everything about every possible object of knowledge in this world. But he has a true knowledge of what his salvation and his reconciliation with God mean and imply. The Christian, Paul stated to the Corinthians, has "the mind of Christ" (1 Cor 2:16). In the life in the Spirit in which he lives, and because of the ministry of the Holy Spirit to him, he begins to see and understand things as Christ does. He has a new understanding of who God is, as the God of grace with whom he now has fellowship. He begins to see the Person of Christ for who he is, he sees sin for what it is, and he sees the scope of the salvation that Christ accomplished for him and the guarantee of eternal life with Christ for what it is.

It is clear that the unction or anointing of the Holy Spirit that John is speaking of here is the property of all Christians by reason of the very fact that they are Christians. There is no other way in which the Christian could have any true knowledge of the things of God. For as Paul the apostle has made clear, "The natural man receiveth not the things of the Spirit of God; for they are foolishness unto him; neither can he know them, because they are spiritually discerned" (1 Cor 2:14).

In the light of all that has been said, in the light of the nature of the union, its source and origin, the reason for its being, and the divine purposes and intentions that it fulfills, the union with Christ is indissoluble. Christ himself has said of the sheep he came to save: "I give unto them eternal life; and they shall never perish, neither shall any man pluck them out of my hand" (John 10:28). The union is indissoluble in that it will be maintained by the grace of God until, and throughout, eternity. But more particularly, it is indissoluble because it is a substantial union with Christ by his Spirit, the breaking of which would imply nothing less than the dismemberment of the relation between Christ and his people that was established definitively in the determinate counsel of God. To say that the union was dissoluble would be to dismember the body of Christ. Christ cannot be divided. And now that he has been joined in substantial and spiritual union with his people, the Christ-church union that exists cannot be divided.

We may anticipate some aspects of what is involved for the believer by virtue of the union with Christ that has thus been sovereignly established. Wilhelmus à Brakel has observed that "This union is therefore real, essential, true, complete, without any reservation, eternally inseparable, spiritual."[4] The Scriptural data are copious. "Know ye not that ye are the temple of God, and that the Spirit of God dwelleth in you?" (1 Cor 3:16). Of the beneficiary of the union it is said that "My Father will love him, and we will come unto him, and make our abode with him" (John 14:23). "He that is joined to the Lord is one spirit" (1 Cor 6:17). "[Ye have] put on the Lord Jesus Christ" (Rom 13:14). "Rooted and built up in him [Christ]" (Col 2:7). "That they also may be one in us . . . I in them" (John 17:21, 23). "Know ye not your own selves, how that Jesus Christ is in you" (2 Cor 13:5). "For as many of you as have been baptized into Christ have put on Christ" (Gal 3:27). "God . . . hath raised us up together, and made us sit together in heavenly places in Christ Jesus" (Eph 2:4, 6).

The comprehensive significance of our union with Christ is confirmed in the fact that not only were the elect of God chosen in Christ (Eph 1:4), but they were united with him in all the aspects of the work of redemption that he accomplished for them. They were crucified with him (Rom 6:6); "buried with him in baptism, wherein also ye are risen with him" (Col 2:12); and as John Murray has observed, believers have fallen asleep in Christ and will rise in Christ (1 Thess 4:14, 16), and with Christ they will be glorified (Rom 8:17).[5] Further, union with Christ involves union with the three Persons of the Godhead. Staggering as the thought and realization may be, it would diminish the very meaning of our salvation to overlook the fact that the mystical union we are now addressing carries with it nothing less than union with the triune Persons of God the Father, God the Son, and God the Holy Spirit. Without a careful recognition of the terms of that union it is not possible to describe or define the Christian person and the eternal prospects and inheritance that he enjoys.

The noted Scottish Reformed theologian of the mid-nineteenth century, James Buchanan, addressed the question then current as to whether our union with Christ is "a union of representation" or a "union of identity."[6] It is more than the former and less than the latter. The believer's union with Christ does not amount to or imply the divinization of man. It is not, and cannot be, a union of identity. Union with Christ does not involve the communication to the individual of the essential properties of the Godhead. It does not convey to the new-born sinner any of the incommunicable attributes of God. But being more than a union of representation it is a real and

---

4. à Brakel, *Christian's Reasonable Service*, 2:89.
5. Murray, *Redemption*, 203–204.
6. Buchanan, *Justification*, 159.

vital and spiritual union. Because Christ is our representative head, against our prior representation by Adam, our union with Christ may be said to be in that sense one of representation. But more than representation is involved. For the believer, in his new life in union with Christ, is the beneficiary of the residence within him of the Holy Spirit whom Christ has sent.

In his high priestly prayer, our Lord prayed in regard to the union of believers with himself: "I in them" (John 17:23); and the apostle John, at the conclusion of his extended argument that the Christian's highest good resides in his "fellowship with the Father, and with his Son Jesus Christ," returns to the point: "We are of God . . . and we are *in* him that is true, even *in* his Son Jesus Christ" (1 John 5:19–20, italics added). The old Puritan commentator, Matthew Poole, adduces that same text when he comments on the opening verse of Paul's first letter to the Thessalonians, where the apostle addresses the church as being "*in* God the Father and the Lord Jesus Christ."[7] And for Paul, the "mystery" that moved his very consciousness and preaching was "Christ in you, the hope of glory" (Col 1:27). John Calvin, at the beginning of Book Three of his *Institutes*, addresses the question: "How do we receive those benefits which the Father bestowed on his only-begotten Son—not for Christ's own private use, but that he might enrich poor and needy men?[8] The answer lies in "the secret working of the Spirit."[9] But before the doctrinal exposition can get under way, Calvin establishes a basic principle that reflects his structure of thought from that point on: "We must understand that as long as Christ remains outside of us, and we are separated from him, all that he has suffered and done for the salvation of the human race remains useless and of no value for us."[10] At that point, the classic Reformed doctrine of the Christian believer's union with Christ comes into clear focus.

It has been recognized by numerous theologians, of course, that union with Christ is a very embracive concept and reality. John Murray observes that "union with Christ is in itself a very broad and embracive subject."[11] He traces the reality of it back to "the eternal election of the Father," and the fact that election, it is clearly stated, is "in Christ."[12] "He hath chosen us

---

7. Matthew Poole, Commentary, 3:731–32.
8. John Calvin, *Institutes*, 537.
9. Idem.
10. Idem.
11. Murray, *Redemption*, 201.
12. Ibid., 202.

## The Christian's Benefit in Christ

in him [Christ] before the foundation of the world" (Eph 1:4). And Murray traces out the relevance of union with Christ for all of the phases and stages of redemption in the manner in which John Frame, for example, has done in his recent *Systematic Theology*: "Union with Christ . . . underlies all the works of God in our lives: election, calling, regeneration, faith, justification, adoption, sanctification, perseverance, and glorification."[13]

But notwithstanding such a relation of union with Christ, in its origin and comprehensive meaning and its relevance to all the parts and processes of redemption, it has become almost a commonplace in the declaration of the gospel to speak of "union with Christ by faith." Several questions arise, therefore, as we reflect further upon the relations involved: First, what is to be understood as the meaning of union with Christ on the personal and experiential level; second, when, in that sense, is the union to be understood as established; and third, what is the manner in which the benefits inherent in it accrue to the believer?

To answer those questions we do well to bear in mind two dichotomies that are to influence our construction of doctrine. The first has to do with the difference between God's sovereign ordination of all that in due time comes to pass, on the one hand, and the eventuation in actual time of his sovereign decrees. We distinguish, that is, between the status, or the standing before and in the accounts of God, of the individual person whom the Spirit of God brings to salvific awareness on the one hand, and that individual's experiential consciousness, or his awakening comprehension of the fact and meaning of that status and its implications for life. At that point the question arises in another aspect of what is, in actual fact, accomplished in the soul of a sinner by the Holy Spirit's sovereign work of regeneration. By that work of the Spirit, we have to say with our present context in view, the individual who is the beneficiary of it is joined in union to Christ.

The union with Christ is definitively established at the point, and in the act, of regeneration. But is it not, as we have acknowledged, appropriate to say that the person who is the subject of God's redemptive grace is joined in union with Christ by faith? Our answer is affirmative. But again we ask: what is to be understood by saying that the individual is "joined to Christ by faith?" The answer follows that a thoroughgoing difference exists between the individual's *status* of union with Christ, on the one hand, and his actual realization of it and of its significance. When, then, the expositor, whether Calvin for example in his statements that we previously adduced, or a contemporary

---

13. Frame, *Systematic Theology*, 914.

preacher or teacher, says that we have union with Christ by faith, or, more properly, by Spirit-filled faith, the reference must be understood to be to the result of the action of an individual in confirming in fact and experience what has already been established in the accounts of heaven.

That important point can be clarified by referring to the discussion by the twentieth-century Reformed theologian, Berkhof, of what he terms "The Mystical Union." Berkhof establishes at the beginning that "Subjectively, the union between Christ and believers is effected by the Holy Spirit in a mysterious and supernatural way."[14] That, of course, reflects the conclusion of Calvin with which we began. But then, as Berkhof proceeds to elaborate the meaning and characteristics of the union he reaches the conclusion we have stated: "The initial act is that of Christ *who unites believers to himself by regenerating them* and thus producing faith in them. On the other hand, the believer also *unites himself to Christ* by a conscious act of faith, and continues the union, under the influence of the Holy Spirit, by the constant exercise of faith."[15]

What, then, are we to understand by the statement that we are joined in union with Christ by faith? Clearly, the meaning must be understood to refer to the second half of what Berkhof has stated; namely, the action of the now regenerate individual.

The seventeenth-century confessions of faith bear on the same point. In its answer to the question, "How are we made partakers of the redemption purchased by Christ?" the Westminster Shorter Catechism states that that is accomplished "by the effectual application of it to us by his Holy Spirit."[16] That is effected by the Spirit's "working faith in us, and thereby *uniting us to Christ* in our effectual calling."[17] The *uniting to Christ* is there conceived of as an aspect of what is involved in God's effectual calling of the sinner to salvation. The matter has been taken further, however, by the *Savoy Declaration of Faith*, the Congregational confession of 1658 that followed and substantially adhered to the *Westminster Confession of Faith* of 1647. Both of those important documents include chapter 13, "Of Sanctification." The Savoy refers there to "[Those] that are effectually called and regenerated, *being united to Christ*."[18] The italicized phrase, which

---

14. Berkhof, *Systematic Theology*, 447.
15. Ibid., 450, italics added.
16. Westminster Shorter Catechism, Question 29.
17. Ibid., Question 30, italics added.
18. *Savoy Declaration of Faith*, XIII:I, italics added.

associates union with Christ with the act of regeneration, is omitted from the *Westminster Confession,* and its inclusion in the Savoy is an example of the keenness of perception among the seventeenth-century Puritans as to the comprehensive import of union with Christ. Further examination will show that both the confessional documents we have referred to, in their parallel chapters on God's eternal decrees, effectual calling, adoption, and sanctification, hold a similarly high view of the determinative import of union with Christ.

The important Dutch Reformed theologian, à Brakel, who was prominent in the Dutch Second Reformation in the seventeenth century, grasped the same conception of the effects of the grace of regeneration. He observes in relation to the beneficiaries of that grace, "Their mind, will, and affections have been changed. They have become new creatures . . . in consequence of this change wrought within the soul."[19] "When the moment of good pleasure arrives for each of the elect . . . the Holy Spirit quickens and grants him spiritual life, *this being the consequence of the soul's union with God in Christ.*"[20] In that statement two quite distinct things are being said. First, it is stated there that there is the close association between regeneration and union with Christ that we have referred to. But second, it is clarified in the italicized phrase that union with Christ is not to be understood properly as the *result* of regeneration, but as the accompanying reality, or rather, as the more remote and embracive action of God from which all aspects and elements of salvation flow.

John Owen, a foremost English language theologian of the same century, effectively made a similar point. "No person, therefore, whatever, who hath not been made partaker of the washing of regeneration and the renovation of the Holy Ghost, can possibly have any union with Christ."[21] Owen continues, by way of clarifying that statement: "I do not speak of this as though our purifying were in order of time and nature antecedent unto our union with Christ, for indeed it is an effect thereof."[22] There is a sense, Owen says, in which regeneration is an "effect" of our union with Christ. In the purpose and provision of God, that is to say, the believer's union with Christ is the comprehensive reality that informs and determines all of the elements and aspects of the salvation of God's elect. In further com-

19. à Brakel, *Christian's Reasonable Service*, 1:183.
20. Idem. Italics added.
21. Owen, *Pneumatologia*. In *Works*, 3:464.
22. Idem.

ments on the "work of the Spirit of God upon our regeneration," Owen states that "This is that whereby we have *union with Jesus Christ*, the head of the church. Originally and *efficiently* the Holy Spirit dwelling in him and us is the cause of this union; but *formally* the new principle of grace is so."[23]

What, then, follows as the obligations imposed upon those who thus, by God's sovereign grace, have been joined in union to Christ? We shall turn to that important question in what follows. But the answer is encapsulated in the admonition of Paul to the Colossians: "As ye have therefore received Christ Jesus the Lord, so walk ye in him" (Col 2:6). That is the way to all joy and spiritual satisfaction in Christ.

---

23. Ibid., 477–78.

CHAPTER 9

# Adoption

A PRINCIPAL QUESTION THAT has arisen many times in our studies, often implicitly as well as directly, is that of what, precisely, is to be understood as the effects of the Holy Spirit's work of regeneration in the soul of a sinner? A more expansive discussion would be at careful lengths to locate regeneration in the entire process of the application of redemption, in what is generally referred to as the *ordo salutis*, in such a way as to maintain consistency with other aspects of biblical doctrine.

We have seen, for example, that because of the human condition of bondage to sin, it is not possible for a person to turn to Christ in saving faith and repentance, unless he is first awakened by the call of God, and unless, by that action of God, faith is created within him. As our Lord himself said, "Except a man be born again, he cannot see the kingdom of God" (John 3:3). The puzzled, perplexed Nicodemus could not on that occasion grasp the meaning of it all. The upshot of the nocturnal encounter that followed was that God the Holy Spirit is sovereign in the communication of his gifts to men. "The wind bloweth where it listeth" (John 3:8). In the order of the application of the benefits of Christ's redemption to those for whom he died, the divine calling and regeneration necessarily precede repentance and faith, the justifying verdict of God that follows, and the sanctification and growth in holiness in the Christian life.

Regeneration, as we discussed aspects of it in the preceding chapter, comes to effect in establishing an individual into union with Christ. That union has inevitably associated with it further blessings. We leave aside for the moment the blessings of the renewal of the faculties of the soul, as that has already been discussed and the significance of that for individual response and Christian behavior. Our concern at this point is with the fact that one's union with Christ is accompanied by the adoption of the repentant sinner as a son into the family of God. Union with Christ and adoption, that is, are necessarily coincident. At his regeneration, one is indissolubly joined in union with Christ (and, we have seen, with the three Persons of the Godhead), and he is adopted as a son of God. Those two inseparable aspects of salvation should be kept in the close relation that defines them. At the point of rescue from the parlous state of sin, at regeneration, the sinner is not only awakened to his true condition of alienation from God. The bounds of grace conveyed to him are limitlessly more extensive. He is made a new person (2 Cor 5:17). The old man, the Adamic man within him, has died. He is given a new nature. He now partakes of the very likeness of God who has communicated new life to him. But further, he is, in fact, adopted into the family of God, and as will become progressively clear to him, he is now the possessor of all the rights and privileges that sonship bestows on him.

The fact and doctrine of adoption is stated liberally in the Scriptures. "When the fullness of the time was come, God sent forth his Son, made of a woman, made under the law, to redeem them that were under the law, that we might receive the *adoption of sons*. And *because ye are sons*, God has sent forth the Spirit of his Son into your hearts, crying, Abba, Father" (Gal 4:4–6, italics added). "Ye have not received the spirit of bondage again . . . but ye have received the Spirit of *adoption*" (Rom 8:15, italics added). "Beloved, now are we the *sons of God* . . . when he shall appear we, shall be like him" (1 John 3:2, italics added). The text is clear; we are adopted as sons of God. Two questions, therefore, press their demands on the Christian believer: First, when is it to be understood that adoption into the sonship of God occurs; and second, what, as a result, are the privileges and obligations that sonship carries with it? We take the first question first.

Recall what has been said regarding the application of salvation and the justification of the believer on the exercise of the gifts of repentance and faith that have been conveyed to him in his regeneration. That justification involves a forensic, declarative statement by God. Justification is forensic in that it effects a definitive change in the believer's status in relation to the law of God. Justification does not, in itself, cause or imply any change in the individual's state of holiness. It is a purely declarative statement by God that whereas previously the individual was *ungodly*, in that he had not kept the law, he is now pronounced in the accounting of God to be *godly*, because the fact that Christ kept the law on his behalf has been imputed to him and placed to his account. "Christ died for the ungodly" (Rom 5:6). The change in state that renders the person holy is referable not to his justification but to his regeneration. Justification is simply and purely forensic, a declarative, forensic statement by God.

At the point of regeneration the individual to whom the grace of God has come is rendered holy in that he is set apart for God who has called him. That act of God has involved the transference of the individual from the kingdom of darkness to the kingdom of God's dear Son. But while the new-born person is now holy in that intrinsic, essential, sense of separateness from what previously described his sinful state, he remains ungodly. By that it is meant that notwithstanding his new separation from his old estate to God, and notwithstanding the renewal of his person that the regenerating grace of God has accomplished in him, he is still, in the sight of God, in the position that he is ungodly. He is ungodly by virtue of the fact that he has not kept the law of God in the perfect obedience that the law and the righteousness of God demand. In having failed to honor the law of God with integrity and completeness, he has repudiated the covenantal obligations that were laid upon him. For that is the meaning of sin at its most basic level and significance. Sin is the repudiation of covenantal obligations.

What, then, needs to be done? It is necessary that at that point God should constitute the repentant sinner righteous, or, that is, godly. He does that by placing the forensic righteousness of Christ to his account. God gives the sinner the forensic righteousness of Christ. It is his new possession. It is the *forensic* righteousness of Christ because it is the righteousness that accrued to Christ by virtue of his having kept the law of God perfectly. At that point the promise contained in the exaltation of the prophet Isaiah of old has been fulfilled: "I will greatly rejoice in the LORD ... for he hath clothed me with the garments of salvation, he hath covered me with the robe of righteousness" (Isa 61:10). That being done according to the grace of God, the sinner is now declared to be himself just and righteous. At that point God's statement of justification is a declarative, forensic statement that settles the sinner's new estate in Christ once and for all.

Given, then, that justification is a forensic act of God, what is to be said of the believer's adoption, his adoption into the family of God that follows God's calling and regenerating arrest of him? Are we to understand that God's act of adoption is also essentially forensic, that its explanation is to be found primarily in its implied change in legal status? The question may appear to be settled in John Murray's observation that "Adoption is, like justification, a judicial act.... It is the bestowal of a status, or standing, not the generating within us of a new nature or character."[1] Such a statement might be thought to imply that emphasis should fall on the forensic significance of the act of adoption. But Murray, though he insists that adoption is to be distinguished from both justification and regeneration and "is much more than either or both of these acts of grace,"[2] goes on to observe that "There is a close relation between adoption and regeneration."[3] "There is a very close interdependence between the generative act of God's grace (regeneration) and the adoptive."[4] That is the point that has now to be emphasized in order to see what adoption is in its objective sense.

What is at issue, as will become clear as our discussion proceeds, is whether we are to understand adoption as primarily a forensic benefit, or, that is, a status resulting from a forensic statement of God comparable to, or, as some theologians state, following from, the corresponding forensic statement of justification. R. C. Sproul, for example, has recently concluded that "We are children of God by adoption, *which is a fruit of our justification.*"[5] Sproul goes on to say, "In our adoption as sons, we also enjoy the mystical union of the believer with Christ."[6] If, then, as has just been said, adoption is a "fruit" of justification, and if, further, "In our adoption we enjoy union with Christ," are we to understand that our union with Christ is also a fruit of our justification? It is clear that some sorting out of the relations between these blessings that accrue to us is seriously necessary.[7]

The linkage of adoption with justification has, of course, a long heritage. Sproul's statement echoes what became a predominant motif in theological doctrine following the work of Francis Turretin, Calvin's successor in Geneva. In his *Elenctic Theology* Turretin asks "What is the adoption *which is given to us in justification?*"[8] And he goes on to state that "The other part

---

1. Murray, *Redemption*, 166.
2. Ibid., 165.
3. Ibid., 166.
4. Idem.
5. Sproul, *Everyone's a Theologian*, 245, italics added.
6. Idem.
7. It is worthy of note that Sproul's focus on justification is further expressed in his statement: "The moment we are justified, a real change is enacted upon us by the Holy Spirit, so that we are increasingly brought into conformity with Christ. The change of our nature toward holiness and righteousness begins immediately," ibid., 247. The question arises whether "the change of nature" begins, as Sproul has it, at justification or at the sinner's prior regeneration.
8. Turretin, *Institutes*, 2:666, italics added.

of justification is adoption or the bestowal of a right to life, flowing from Christ's righteousness, which acquired for us not only deliverance from death, but also a right to life by the adoption with which he endows us."[9] Thus there entered into Reformed theology the assumption that adoption was to be understood, in its primary sense, as closely associated with, if not entirely determined by, God's forensic declarations. That emphasis, as we shall see, may appear on the surface to have been also the primary emphasis on the point of the seventeenth-century confessions.[10]

The question has continued whether a primarily forensic element is to be foremost in the explanation of adoption, or whether its relational and explicitly familial significance, as that is established by the new birth, is to be considered prominent. Douglas Kelly is undoubtedly correct in his regretting the "narrowing down of the crucial relationship of redeemed humans to the Holy God into only forensic terms."[11] Our own conclusion, that brings the issue of adoption into relation with the Holy Spirit's sovereign work of regeneration, is aimed to establish in clearer perspective the familial realities of adoption, and to insist that what is involved in that conveyance of grace is, in fact, the establishment of a new nature and character in the one adopted. Herman Witsius among the earlier Reformed theologians pointed to the same conclusion. He saw adoption as "a right to the inheritance," and "the elect . . . become the sons of God by a new and spiritual generation."[12]

The conveyance to the sinner of the grace of regeneration involves a change in moral nature, while adoption in itself involves the establishment of a new and living relation between God and the regenerate believer. The experiential living out of that relation has to do with the subjective and ongoing benefits of adoption, as distinct from the objective reality of adoption that we are here addressing. In what is said in the following regarding the relation between regeneration and adoption we shall not be saying that regeneration *is* adoption, but, as we have observed, there comes to effect

---

9. Idem.

10. The frequently-observed lack of attention to the doctrine of adoption by the English Puritans and their successors has been substantially corrected by Beeke, in "The Puritans on Adoption," in Beeke and Jones, *Puritan Theology*, 537–54.

11. Kelly, "Adoption," in *Reformed Theological Review*, 112, cited in Trumper, *When History Teaches Us Nothing*, 6. See Trumper, op. cit., for an extended response to the recent Sonship debate.

12. Witsius, *Economy of the Covenants*, 442, 444.

at regeneration the individual's adoption into the family of God. A filial relation is established at that point in a critically important objective sense.

We have it in Galatians 4:5 that Christ redeemed us in order that "we might receive the adoption of sons [or as sons]," or, in the instance we are now considering, the adoption that properly belongs to sons. It is as sons that we are adopted, with full rights to all the privileges and benefits of sonship. And at the same time we have received also "the Spirit of adoption" (Rom 8:15), who applies to us the realization of the benefits and privileges that adoption implies. God gives the believer both the new status of adoption into sonship and the "Spirit of adoption" who makes that status meaningful and operative in the life of the believer.

Adoption, then, associated with the believer's regeneration, is seen as integral to the complex of God's actions in relation to the complete application of redemption. God the Father does not adopt us to make us sons. Because, according to his eternal ordination, he "gave us power to become the sons of God" (John 1:12), he has adopted us *as* sons. *We are not sons because we have been adopted. We have been adopted because God has made us sons.*

The distinction is frequently drawn, in our present day social context, between one who is a son in a certain family by natural birth, and one who has been transferred to become a son of a different family by adoption. In the eyes of the law, the one who has been adopted has a right to all the benefits and privileges of membership of the family into which he has been adopted. In that way, the law is casting its judgment on the case, and that means that the forensic aspect of the adoption is predominant. But in the case we have under examination, namely adoption into the family of God, that legal principle and relationship should not be allowed to assume initial prominence. For it must be understood that as to the matter of sonship of God, the Christian believer, who has a right to all the benefits and privileges of membership of the family of God, is *a son by birth*. That is the critical factor in the case. The Christian believer is a son of God by birth because he has been born again by the Spirit of God. And because his status as a son turns in that manner on the new identity that the Holy Spirit of God produces within him, the individual now partakes of the nature of his heavenly Father. It is precisely that emergence, by the grace and by the fact of regeneration, of the very nature of God that is thereby conveyed to the sinner that raises the identity of sonship far above that of a mere forensic relationship. Nothing less than what has now been stated is involved in the

Holy Spirit's conveyance to God's chosen people of the grace of regeneration. That is why John can say "We are the sons of God" (1 John 3:2).

The necessary linkage of the doctrine and fact of our adoption to the reality of regeneration has been well stated by Joel Beeke: "*When we are born again,* Christ delivers us from Satan's slavery, and ... transfers us to the Father's sonship.... The Holy Spirit changes us from children of wrath, which we are by nature, into children of God *by means of regeneration,* or the new birth, sealing our adoption with His own witness."[13] In his *Heirs with Christ* Beeke observes in his "acknowledgments" that "I owe thanks ... to the glorious God and Father for adopting me ... objectively, through regenerating me."[14] Candlish observes: "Literally and truly he [God] begets us as children to himself."[15] And then, because we are the sons of God, we are "joint-heirs with Christ" (Rom 8:16–17).

We observe, then, why the analogy between human family adoption and the Christians' adoption as sons of God is finally not sustainable. The breakdown of the analogy turns on the nature of the person adopted. In the human family case the child adopted does not share the nature of the family into which he has come. His essential nature is forever alien. He is regarded as a member of the family only because of a legal assumption. In the eyes of the law, that is, he now has the right to all of the privileges and responsibilities of the family into which he has been adopted. But in the matter of the Christians' adoption as sons of God, focusing, as has been said, on the nature of the person who is adopted, the case is entirely different. In the latter case the individual is a son by birth. That is to say, being born again, he does, by that very act of birth, partake of the same nature as God whose son he now is, born anew by the creation within him of a new heavenly nature by the Spirit of God. As to that act of being born again, or regeneration, Beeke again sums up the reality of adoption in the following terms: "We are not what we once were (1 John 3:9). God has done what no human father and mother can do when they adopt a child—change the personality and the nature of the child they have adopted so that it is like theirs. But God, in regeneration, has allowed his born-again children to become partakers

---

13. Beeke, "The Apostle John," in Beeke, *Beauty and Glory of the Father,* 86, 89, italics added.

14. Beeke, *Heirs with Christ,* xv. On the relation between regeneration and adoption see also the articles on "Regeneration" and "Adoption" in Beeke et al., *KJV Study Bible,* 1774 and 1628.

15. Candlish, *Commentary,* 2:193.

of His own loving, holy nature as their Father in heaven."[16] And "When we are born again, God delivers us from Satan's enslaving family and, by His astounding grace, transfers us to the Father's sonship. He calls us sons; we are adopted into his family."[17]

The apostle Peter pressed the reality on his readers by his statement that the person whom God has thus brought to himself is a "partaker of the divine nature" (2 Pet 1:4). Of course Peter is not saying that the newborn person has now partaken of the essence of the Godhead, or that in some mystic sense he has been absorbed into that essence. We observed previously that regeneration does not involve the divinization of man. The Christian is a partaker of the divine nature in the sense that now, to the degree specified by the sovereign counsel and will of God, the communicable attributes of God have been communicated to him.

Of course it is true that the human analogy of adoption is relevant in the respect that whereas the person who is adopted was once a child of his "father the devil" (John 8:44), he has been transferred to the family of God.[18] The individual is transferred from one family, that of the devil, to another, that of God. In that sense there is a forensic aspect to adoption as we are now considering it. But that does not permit or require the conclusion that the Christian's adoption is principally or primarily a matter of God's forensic declaration. Certainly the law of God comes to relevance in the ongoing life of the individual. The law in its moral aspect is his rule of life. But what is to be said on that level, as to the subjective realization of the benefits of adoption, is quite distinct from the reality of adoption in and of itself.

To see further what is involved, reflect on the state of man as he came from the hands of his creator. He was, we have said, the image of God. It was not that God created man and then imposed his image on him, so that he could then be said to be God's image-bearer. We say, rather, that man as he was created *is* the image of God. We put that previously by saying that as to both his being and his knowledge man is the analogue of God. That means that he is like God in every respect in which a finite entity can be like his infinite creator. Man as created was *like* God, though he was not *identical* with God. That is the meaning of the fact that he was the analogue of God.

---

16. Beeke, *Heirs with Christ*, 26.

17. Ibid., 41.

18. See Colossians 1:13 for God's definitive transference of the believer "from the power of darkness . . . into the kingdom of his dear Son."

## Adoption

Now that by regeneration the entailment of sin has been broken, the individual who is the beneficiary of that grace is again like his creator, his heavenly Father. The effects of the fall have been reversed. Indeed we know that, as a result of regeneration, man is raised to a higher state than that from which Adam fell. "Where sin abounded, grace did much more abound" (Rom 5:20). And the "more abounded," the higher estate to which the regenerate child of God is raised, is that now he is joined to Christ in, as we have said, an organic, vital, spiritual, and indissoluble union. Adam was not joined to Christ in that sense.

The fact that the new-born Christian is to be understood as a *son of God by birth*, having thereby the very nature of God who by his Spirit has occasioned that birth, is emphasized by our Lord himself when he said "Ye must be *born* again" (John 3:7). The new nature that the child of God now possesses is the analogue of, and is connoted by a likeness to, the nature of God who has created that new life within him.[19]

Before leaving the subject of the doctrine of adoption it will be well to refer to our confessional statement on the point. The Presbyterian *Westminster Confession of Faith* of 1647, the Congregationalist *Savoy Declaration of Faith* of 1658, and the Baptist *Second London Confession* of 1689 are unanimous in their wording on the doctrine of adoption. It is stated that "All those that are justified, God vouchsafeth, in and for his only Son Jesus Christ, to make partakers of the grace of adoption; by which they are taken into the number, and enjoy the liberties and privileges of the children of God." Two questions arise: first, the reference to justification at the beginning of that statement may raise the question whether the grace of adoption, as it is administered in actual time, is to be understood as consequent upon the declaration of justification; and second, whether, following that, adoption is to be understood as primarily a forensic concept, as is justification

---

19. Considerable discussion of the doctrine of adoption has occurred recently in connection with critiques of what became known as the *Sonship* theology. See Trumper op. cit. for his suggestion that the doctrine of adoption calls for development in a redemptive-theological context. He sees the classic biblical texts in the following manner: Ephesians 1:4–5 speaks to Protology, Romans 9:4 to Covenant Theology, Galatians 4:4–5 to Soteriology, Romans 8:15–16 to Pneumatology, and Romans 8:22–23 to Eschatology, op. cit., 85. In the light of our suggestion that adoption is to be seen as an effect of, or associated with, regeneration, it can be noted that Trumper, at op. cit., 84, argues that "the biblical data cautions us against the Puritan practice of conflating Paul's adoption model with other filial models of the New Testament, notably John's new birth model." Clearly a careful sorting out of the relevant doctrinal loci is called for. We have endeavored to contribute to that highly desirable end.

itself. In short, is our understanding of adoption as coming to effect at the point of regeneration, and as associated with regeneration in the manner we have suggested, contradicted by the confessional statements?

No contradiction is necessarily involved. The confessions, in the statements they have made, do not have to be read as addressing the time at which the grace of adoption is conveyed. They properly advance the claim that the ground upon which that grace becomes the property of those who are justified is, as is the case with all of the blessings implicit in redemption, the salvific work of Christ, as that issues in the justification of sinners.

Further, we bear in mind, in our articulation of doctrine, that a difference should frequently be seen to exist between *real* distinctions and *intellectual* distinctions. By that I mean that we make very proper distinctions between the temporal stages or processes of the *application* of redemption (for example calling, regeneration, justification, sanctification etc.), or the *ordo salutis*, when the blessings themselves are not necessarily sequentially temporal in character. For example, in the *ordo salutis* we treat sanctification only after regeneration, and further, only after justification, whereas sanctification in its definitive aspect is properly understood to have begun at regeneration. In a similar way, we speak properly of adoption in its objective sense at the point of regeneration, though with equal propriety much is to be said at a later point regarding the application of the benefits of adoption.

As we have mentioned already, we have spoken throughout of adoption in an *objective* sense as being an effect of regeneration. We have not addressed the subjective aspects of the doctrine; or, in other words, we have not at this stage exhibited in a full sense the benefits that flow from adoption. But there is to be said at this point, as was observed earlier in connection with an individual's realization of salvation, that a difference, and imaginably a lapse of time, exists between the *fact* of one's *entry into life* by regeneration and the personal awareness and appropriation of the blessings involved. Such a difference now applies in the case of adoption. We turn in the following chapter to reflect on the benefits and obligations of the sinner's adoption into the family of God.

CHAPTER 10

# The Imperative of Faith

THE CHRISTIAN LIFE IS life communicated to the sinner by the sovereign and unsolicited grace of God. The Second Person of the eternal Godhead, himself "God blessed for ever" (Rom 9:5), came into the world to become Jesus Christ in order that those whom he came to redeem "might have life, and that they might have it more abundantly" (John 10:10). Writing in his first epistle, the apostle John argues that Christ who came is the very "Word of life" (1 John 1:1), and the life, he says, has been "manifested unto us." The manner of that manifestation has engaged us in the preceding chapters and the realities involved project their significance to the imperatives laid upon those who are the recipients of that life in Christ.

In the preceding two chapters we have looked, all too briefly, at two of the benefits that accrue to those whom God has called to himself, those to whom, by the sovereign work of his Holy Spirit, he has granted the grace of regeneration. Foremost, we have seen, those who are called are joined to God in Christ in an organic, vital, spiritual, and indissoluble union. The union involved implies union with the three divine Persons of the Godhead. That union carries along with it the fact that the people who are thus favored by divine decree are, as we stated it, sons of God by birth. God has made them his sons by the new birth, born again as our Lord stated its necessity in his encounter with Nicodemus. Because they are born of God the Father they naturally partake of the nature and the likeness of the Father. Union with Christ and adoption into the family of God describe the existential character of the Christian's status in its highest degree. Those blessings and benefits provide the entrance to what must be described as the Christian's highest good; namely, as John has stated it, the privilege of "fellowship with the Father" (1 John 1:3). As John stated at the end of his first epistle, we are "in him" and "in his Son Jesus Christ" (1 John 5:20).

## The Divine Purchase

Attached to both those remarkable blessings and benefits are obligations that devolve on the beneficiaries. The Scriptures display liberally what is involved in the imperatives for Christian living. The apostles are in unison in their directives. In the light of the blessings, Peter said, "What manner of persons ought ye to be in all holy conversation [or manner of life] and godliness?" (2 Pet 3:11). Paul admonishes the Christian believers: "Be not conformed to this world; but be ye transformed by the renewing of your mind" (Rom 12:2). And John states the imperative: "Love not the world, neither the things that are in the world. If any man love the world, the love of the Father is not in him" (1 John 2:15). And again Paul sums up the Christian ethic: "As ye have therefore received Christ Jesus the Lord, so walk ye in him" (Col 2:6). The scriptural directives are copious and well known. But it is necessary, in the context of those blessings themselves, to reflect on, first, the manner in which the consciousness of the scope of the blessings is borne on the Christian's awareness; and second, the imperatives for life that follow from them.

In our meditation on Christian doctrine and its implications for life, it is important to maintain awareness of certain distinctions that we referred to at the end of chapter 9 on "Adoption." We referred there to the fact that an *intellectual* distinction may exist and be properly made, where a *real* distinction may not exist when matters of God's relations with man are concerned. By that it is meant, for example, that in formulating our doctrine we draw an intellectual distinction between, say, regeneration and the ensuing development of the regenerate believer's sanctification. But it would be difficult to insist that a *real* distinction exists, because it must equally properly be said that the believer's sanctification begins at the moment of his regeneration. Some theologians have circumvented that appearance of doctrinal difficulty by referring to *definitive sanctification* as occurring at the time of one's regeneration, and to *progressive sanctification* as referring to the progress of the subsequent development of holiness throughout the Christian's life.[1]

We may put that in a different way. In our discussion of the sinner's adoption as a son of God, we took the position that the repentant sinner is received into the state of sonship and adoption by God at the time of his regeneration. We said that one becomes a son of God by birth, by the new birth that is antecedent to all the blessings of the Christian life. But then

---

1. See Murray, on *definitive sanctification* and *progressive sanctification* in Collected Writings, 2:277–304.

## The Imperative of Faith

a further question arises. The gracious act of God that we have called the new birth is itself an act of God in which the individual has no part at all. He is entirely passive in his regeneration. That act of regeneration involves the communication to the individual of certain benefits, such as the gifts of faith and repentance. Or more particularly, it conveys to the individual the ability to exercise faith that does, in due course, bring the sinner to the cross of Christ and to confession of belief and trust in him. It follows, therefore, that there is, and that there must be, a lapse of time between the act of regeneration and a person's coming to conscious awareness of his new status as a member of the kingdom of God to which, as the Scriptures abundantly declare, he had been translated (Col 1:13). Theologians have addressed in various ways the important fact of that lapse of time.

Consider the words of the distinguished Scottish theologian of the nineteenth century to whom we referred previously, James Buchanan. Referring to regeneration as the renewal of the individual, Buchanan observes that "No man is justified who is not renewed, nor is any man renewed who is not also justified."[2] It is implicit in Buchanan's argument, the details of which cannot be adequately addressed in the present space, that the exercise of faith that leads to justification proceeds with minimal lapse of time beyond the point of regeneration. John Murray appears similarly to contemplate a minimum time-lapse in the same relation. In the spirit of Buchanan's larger analysis, Murray sets regeneration and justification together in the following way: "Regeneration pushes itself into consciousness and expresses itself in the exercise of faith and repentance. It is true that, except a man be regenerated, he cannot enter into the kingdom of God, but it is also just as true that every person regenerated has entered into the kingdom of God."[3] Murray does not discuss explicitly the time between the sovereign endowment of regeneration and the individual's exercise of the faith that has been communicated to him. But it appears that Murray has in view a minimum time.

On the other hand, the important and well-known Dutch theologian Abraham Kuyper holds a very different view. Kuyper draws an analogy between a person's first birth and his second birth, understanding the latter to refer to regeneration. "In the nature of the case, man is unconscious of his first birth. Consciousness comes only with the years. And the same applies

---

2. Buchanan, op. cit., 402. The details of Buchanan's treatment of regeneration and justification are worthy of the closest inspection.

3. Murray, *Collected Writings*, 2:198.

to regeneration, of which he was unconscious until the time of his conversion; and that may be ten or twenty years."[4]

The two questions we have raised, the matter of *real* versus *intellectual* distinctions in the statement of biblical doctrine, and that of the difference between regeneration and an individual's conscious awareness of its reality and effects, are relevant to the two areas of doctrine we have addressed—that of the adoption of an individual into sonship of God, and that of his union with Christ. As to sonship, we distinguish between the reality of one's entry to sonship by the new birth as we have explored that, and the individual's coming to awareness of his sonship status. It is the focus on the latter that has led to the widespread assumption that one is declared to be a son of God only at the point of the expression of faith and therefore at justification. In that way, the fact and doctrine of adoption tends to be considered primarily in forensic terms.

As to the fact and doctrine of the believer's union with Christ, which, we have seen, is established at the point of regeneration, there is again a need to distinguish between the act of establishment itself and a person's conscious awareness of his new status. The twentieth-century Reformed theologian, Berkhof, has addressed that relation as follows: "The initial act [of establishing union with Christ] is that of Christ, *who unites believers to himself by regenerating them* and thus producing faith in them. On the other hand, the believer also *unites himself to Christ* by a conscious act of faith, and continues the union, under the influence of the Holy Spirit, by the constant exercise of faith."[5] The focus on the latter part of Berkhof's statement, that the believer, by reaction to the work that the Spirit of God has done within him, has united himself to Christ, leads to the widespread doctrinal statement that we have union with Christ by faith.

Against the background of the doctrines we have inspected, the questions arise of the benefits enjoyed by the Christian believer and the responsibilities and obligations imposed upon him. The first thing to be said is that we are speaking of covenantal benefits and obligations. At the beginning of our studies we observed in outline form the general character of the covenantal relations that God has established. A prominent part of all of God's covenants is that they each contain promises and obligations. It is not necessary to recall the detail to observe that the covenant of grace that God the Father made with his people as represented by Christ contains both

---

4. Kuyper, *Work of the Holy Spirit*, 288.
5. Berkhof, *Systematic Theology*, 450, italics added.

## The Imperative of Faith

promises and obligations. Moreover, as the covenant of grace is understood as an implementing covenant established in order to realize the objectives of the covenant of redemption between the Persons of the Godhead before the foundation of the world, promises and obligations attach to it so far as both the Person of Christ on the one hand, and his people on the other, are concerned. The promise to God the Son, who voluntarily became the redeemer and federal head of his people, was that in ways we have already seen he would be rewarded for his faithful completion of his messianic-redemptive assignment. But it is equally clear that while the covenant of grace was not, of course, a conditional covenant on our part, in that the accomplishment of our salvation turns entirely on the grace of God and not on any merit or work that we could offer, the covenant was conditional in that respect on the part of Christ. He did, in fact, faithfully and completely fulfill all the conditions and obligations laid upon him.

But now that the redemption of the Christian believer is sure, it having been irrevocably accomplished by the faithfulness of Christ, the obligation is laid upon the Christian to walk in this life in obedience to the law that God has set forth as the rule of life. The law that God gave to his people of old in the earlier form of administration of the covenant of grace has been fulfilled by Christ, and it has passed away as to its ceremonial and civil forms. But the law in its moral aspect, or the moral law as summarized in the Ten Commandments that God gave to Moses, remains obligatory on the Christian. The mandates of that law spread their influence to every aspect of the Christian's life. That, then, establishes the obligation of the Christian person under the covenant of grace, not an obligation to any performance that could merit redemption, but obligation to live in holiness and righteousness before God.

Reflect for a moment on what has been said regarding the personhood of the Christian believer, as that has been established by the grace of regeneration, adoption into the family of God, and union with Christ. Adoption followed from the fact that at the point of his regeneration the new life that the believer received not only transferred him from the kingdom of Satan and sin to the kingdom of God, but it endowed him with the very likeness of God whose son he now is. That is displayed in the sense that because the believer is a son of God by birth, by the new birth, he is inevitably like the Father whose son he is and who breathed that new life into him. We saw that that likeness in nature to the Father differentiated his adoption from the forensic adoption of an individual into a different family in the ordinary cultural complex of the world. In the light of those realities, the obligation on the Christian is to live consistently with the character of holiness that he now possesses.

The Christian's sonship of God in his union with Christ casts wide the benefits and privileges he now enjoys. God, by his regenerating grace, has given to the believer "the mind of Christ" (1 Cor 2:16), so that he begins to see things as God himself in Christ sees them—the knowledge of the being and character of God, the glory of the Person of Christ, the meaning of sin, the scope of redemption, and all that follows from that. Those benefits accrue on the basis of our faith, as the renewal of the mind and heart, and thereby the ability to exercise faith, is a gift of the Holy Spirit. The relationship between God in his triune being and the Christian person has a transforming effect on and in the believer that enables him to say with Paul in Galatians 2:20, "Christ liveth in me." It is transforming in that God has made us "partakers of the divine nature" (2 Peter 1:4). By that it is meant that God by his Spirit conveys to us, or establishes in us, aspects of his communicable attributes. In the course of his sanctifying influence on and within us he does that in the degree and to the extent that he is preparing us for the place he has ordained we shall occupy in his eternal kingdom of glory. It is a relationship that because of its spiritual intimacy is a thing of abounding joy, as Peter puts it: "Ye rejoice with joy unspeakable and full of glory" (1 Peter 1:8).

But beyond those transforming effects, the Christian enjoys the high privilege of access to the very throne room of heaven. As he raises his prayer to the Father he is conscious that he can come to him with a confidence and boldness, and with an openness that only a "son" of God can know and enjoy. He can know with unsullied assurance that his heavenly Father knows all about him and waits to hear his "son's" worship and praise, and to hear his needs and petitions. He knows that his Father is his sure retreat in every storm, a rescue from the gales and cares of his life. But more than that, the Christian knows, by virtue of his innermost conviction and awareness of it, that his Father has declared his love for him, an everlasting love, born of divine will from all eternity, that will never fail nor change. The Christian knows, with an assurance that the gates of hell cannot destroy though they may attempt to shake it, that the Father has again and again arrested and given to him the testimony of the Holy Spirit that he is, in truth, a child of his heavenly Father.

## The Imperative of Faith

What, we may ask then, is the Christian's highest good, his *summum bonum*? Surely, it is to see God. That is at the heart of the apostle John's perception when he says: "Beloved, now are we the sons of God, and it doth not yet appear what we shall be; but we know that, when he [or it] shall appear, we shall be like him; for *we shall see him* as he is" (1 John 3:2, italics added). The meaning of that textual statement is not exhausted by saying that our seeing him will make us like him. The opposite is in a significant sense true. We shall see him as he is because in this life, by the Holy Spirit's ministry to us, we have been made progressively like him. Matthew Poole, a Puritan commentator, makes the judicious comment at that point that "by that likeness [we are] *qualified* for such a vision" (italics added).[6] While that is so, it remains true that then our holiness will be complete and we will be made perfectly blessed in our transformation into the image of Christ.

In the life to come we shall *see* God in the face of his Son. But is there not *in this life* a *summum bonum*, a highest good, for the Christian? The answer that must follow takes up the precise terms that inform the essential vision of John's epistle. It is that though we cannot *see* God with the eyes of flesh, is possible to *know* God and to have intimate *fellowship with him*. John had said in his gospel, "This is life eternal, that they might *know* thee the only true God" (John 17:3). We are already the sons of God. We are adopted into his family because by his regenerating grace he has made us sons. But we are not sons merely or even primarily in a legal, forensic sense. We are sons who have the high privilege of entrance into the very throne room of the Father. For "Through him [Christ] we both [Jews and Gentiles] have access by one Spirit unto the Father" (Eph 2:18).

But doctrine, the high doctrines that elucidate the benefits the Christian has by virtue of his "fellowship with the Father" (1 John 1:3), is the parent of practice. As the apostle explained to the Ephesians, the objective and purpose of our redemption is that "we should be to the praise of his glory" (Eph 1:12). "Ye are a chosen generation," Peter observed in his first epistle, "a peculiar people; that ye should show forth the praises of him who hath called you out of darkness into his marvellous light" (1 Pet 2:9). The scriptural data could be multiplied. The covenant of redemption clearly lays inescapable obligations on those who are the beneficiaries of it. There is an "oughtness" that clearly accompanies the benefits mandated to us by reason of our redemption by the Christ of the covenant. "Ye ought to walk and to please God," Paul says to the Thessalonians, "for this is the will of God, even

---

6. Poole, op. cit., 934.

your sanctification" (1 Thess 4:1–3). We are to be pleasing before him who has chosen us in Christ (Eph 1:4). It is precisely at that point that the moral law as the rule of life for God's people comes into relevance and focus.

The imperatives of the moral law may be alternatively summarized in the following manner. The apostle John has spoken at length of what he sees as defining the character of the persons who, as he had stated at the beginning of his letter, have been raised to the privilege of "fellowship with the Father." He addresses those character distinctives under what we may refer to as *moral, social, and intellectual* headings. John's letter is worthy of the closest inspection and study. We observe briefly that by "moral" reference is made to the keeping of God's commandments. "Social" refers explicitly to the relationship of love that exists between the people of God as they have fellowship with him. And "intellectual" reminds us that the Christian life is above all an intelligent life. That opens up a high level of meaning and significance of the Christian life. As all the faculties of soul, mind, emotions, and will, or the intellectual, affective, and volitional faculties are engaged as the individual turns to God in repentance and saving faith, so all the faculties are engaged in fellowship with God and in conduct and behavior in the Christian life. In his epistle John says repeatedly that "we know" certain things (1 John 2:3, 2:13–14, 2:21, 3:19, 5:19–20). Christianity is a "we know" religion. For the regenerate Christian the mind has become again the prince of the faculties of the soul, the place of hegemony it occupied before Adam's fall. The first appeal of the gospel and the call to repentance is an appeal to the mind. The very meaning of the word "repent" is "think again." That appeal is heard and responded to by the mind that has been renewed by the regenerating grace of God; and the mind, now enlightened and understanding what God has revealed and declared, now perceiving things that were previously hidden by the blindness of mind (2 Cor 4:4) that Satan had imposed, will be paramount in guiding the Christian person to Christ. Similarly, the Christian person will be guided, by the engagement of all his faculties of soul, in his fulfillment of the obligations under the covenant of grace.

The imperatives of faith bear close relation to the question of the Christian's progress in sanctification. Holding to the sovereignty of God in sanctification, the definition of the Catechism is apposite: "Sanctification is the work of God's free grace whereby we are renewed in the whole man after the image of God, and are enabled more and more to die unto sin, and live unto righteousness."[7] There is wisdom in the old theological definition that whereas justification is an "*act* of God's free grace," sanctification is an on-going process or a "*work* of God's free grace."[8] Recalling previous categories, in justification the righteousness of Christ is *imputed* to the Christian believer, while in sanctification his righteousness is *imparted* to the Christian.

It follows that because God has set apart his people for himself and brings his Spirit to bear on their progress in holiness and likeness to him, they are to recognize their status as joined to Christ and for that reason to sanctify themselves. The directive is clear: "work out your own salvation," that is, work out the meaning, the blessings, the obligation, and the prospects of it, "with fear and trembling. For it is God which worketh in you both to will and to do of his good pleasure" (Phil 2:12–13). The injunction is repeated in the Scriptures, as on the occasion when Joshua said to the people: "Sanctify yourselves; for tomorrow the LORD will do wonders among you" (Josh 3:5); or when God said to Moses in the context of the Levitical law: "Sanctify yourselves therefore, and be ye holy; for I am the LORD your God. . . . I am the LORD which sanctify you" (Lev 20:7–8).

In the Christian's sanctification the same principle comes to effect in a twofold way. First, it is God who sanctifies us, sets us apart for his own use and glory and purpose; and second, we who know ourselves to be his people are therefore called upon to sanctify ourselves, to be careful to set ourselves apart from all that we know to be contrary to his holy character and inconsistent with his precepts and law. The necessity of the Christian's separation from his sinful state is what we can refer to as the *objective* necessity of sanctification. The *subjective* necessity is addressed to the Christian's personal and individual responsibility to pursue holiness in the manner we have seen. It is necessary not only that the Christian should be set apart for God and granted new standing in relation to him, but that the righteousness of Christ should be formed within the individual person. It is necessary that he should be gradually changed in the totality of his being in such a way that he should be like Christ, as Christ himself was in all aspects of his character in complete conformity to the law of God.

When we speak of the subjective necessity of sanctification we have in view not only the actual process of renewal itself, but also the fact that the Christian needs to know for himself, within himself and subjectively, that

---

7. Westminster Shorter Catechism, Question 35.
8. Ibid., Questions 33–35.

that process is at work and effective. He needs to know that truly, subjectively, and clearly, because he is told to "follow peace . . . and the holiness, without which," the writer to the Hebrews states, "no man shall see the Lord" (Heb 12:14).

The imperatives that thus direct the Christian life are clear. But the Christian sins. What, then, is to be said of sin in the life of the Christian and its relation to the objective of which we have spoken?

Of the fact of the believer's sin there can be no doubt. The experiences of the saints bear witness to it, as certainly as the Scriptures envisage it. Indeed, it is the most advanced saint who is more conscious of the sin that still clings to him and into which he is ever in danger of falling, apart from the sustaining and preserving grace of God. For sin is not a light matter. As the new-born man of God advances in grace he will progressively realize the true meaning of the sinfulness of sin, and the fact that his best works and thoughts and imaginations are tainted by sin. And when the regenerate man is aware of sin he will, he must, flee from it.

Recalling our previous conclusions regarding the state of Christian personhood, we can summarize the reasons for sin in the life of the Christian. First, as a result of the Holy Spirit's work that has made the person a Christian person, all of his faculties of soul have been endowed with abilities and capacities they did not previously possess. That is the fundamental sense in which he is a new person. He is characterized by a new nature. But second, the faculties have not yet been perfected in holiness. They are new. They are holy in that they are capable of genuinely holy action. They are such that the man cannot ever be what he was before. He is now joined to Christ and he has the life of Christ coursing within him. But because the faculties have not yet been perfected in holiness there remains in the soul what must be recognized as *residual inclinations to sin*. That is what Paul referred to in the second half of the seventh chapter of his letter to the Romans. He referred to it as "sin that dwelleth in me," and as the "law of sin in my members" (Rom 7:17, 23). While the progress in holiness continues, therefore, the man himself is capable of being misled by the temptations of the world and the guiles of Satan. The enemy of our souls can appeal to, and elicit a response from, the *residual inclinations to sin*. The mind of the Christian can still be bombarded by the subtle suggestions of Satan and sin. The Christian can still be trapped into remembering the pleasures of sin. Satan can appeal to old emotional satisfactions, and the still imperfectly developed faculties can accede to the suggestions of sin.

## The Imperative of Faith

The regenerate Christian's ability to sin has been put in perspective by the nineteenth-century theologian Robert Dabney as follows: "The new birth *reverses* the moral *habitus* [or disposition or principle of action] of the believer's will, prevalently, but not at first absolutely, and the work of progressive sanctification carries on this change, thus omnipotently begun, towards that absolute completeness which we must possess on entering heaven. In the carnal state, the *habitus* of the sinner's will is absolutely and exclusively godless. In the regenerate state it is prevalently but not completely godly. In the glorified it is absolutely and exclusively godly."[9]

The sadness of our sin is that in falling subject to it we are living below the people that God has made us to be in Christ. Sin in the life of the Christian grieves his Lord to whom he now belongs (Eph 4:30). When the Christian sins he knows he has sinned. He sees ever more clearly, completely, and acutely as he progresses the sinfulness of sin. He knows a sorrow, a remorse, and agony of repentance because of it. And he turns to Christ who alone is able to succor him in his time of stress and weakness (Heb 4:14–16).

While all that is true, the Christian person has an "anchor of the soul" (Heb 6:19), a "place of refuge" (Isa 4:6), a God who is "the rock of my salvation" and the "rock of my refuge" (Ps 89:26, 94:22). He has made gracious provision for us in our pilgrimage in this life. He has made a full provision for our forgiveness and cleansing by the blood of Christ whom he has set forth as a perfect advocate and intercessor for us. Christ in his death is the propitiation for all our sins in his once offering up of himself and thereby providing a sacrifice that does not need to be repeated. The Holy Spirit whom he has sent brings us to repentance and we see afresh the ground of our acceptance with God. The safeguard against sin is then our realization of the position we enjoy in our union with Christ. Because Christ has died for us, we are dead to sin and it no longer has any claim over us. We are freed from the realm, the dominion, and the tyranny of sin, and there is no longer any reason at all why we should serve it.

The imperative implicit in the profession of faith that we have made as God turned our steps to see his salvation in Christ his Son is that we should walk in newness of life before him. Let us note one final mandate that is to determine our life and conduct in the faith we profess. We have it in Paul's first letter to the Corinthians that "whatsoever ye do, do all things to the glory of God" (1 Cor 10:31). But what is "the glory of God?" It is the demonstration of his infinite perfections to all intelligent creatures, in

---

9. Dabney, *Discussions*, 196–97.

heaven and on earth. The Christian's privilege is to be a participant with God in precisely that demonstration. May he grant by his grace that we shall be faithful in obedience to that ultimate imperative that is laid upon us as his redeemed people.

CHAPTER 11

# The Knowledge of God

THE OBJECTIVE OF THIS and the concluding chapter that follows is to look in slightly more depth at the presuppositions that have influenced the substance and determined the order of argument in the preceding chapters. It was stated at the beginning that our two basic presuppositions are first, that *God is*, and second, that *God has spoken*. Those presuppositions form in one aspect the basic apologetic postulates of theological inquiry. The first points to the question of the possibility of knowing God, of having true knowledge of who God is and what he has disclosed as his salvific purpose; and the second raises the question of the manner in which God has, in fact, made himself known. What, then, are the grounds on which the propositions stand and the reasons for their necessity? It is not intended at this point to present an exhaustive argument in either case, and it will be useful to state at the outset two caveats that will restrict the boundaries of what lies ahead.

First, we are not addressing at this point the question that has engaged the philosophers, namely that of whether logical proofs of the existence of God can be established. That has, of course, given rise to a long and, from its own vantage point, an important literature. We have not given space to the familiar so-called theistic proofs, for example the ontological proof that goes back to Anselm in the eleventh century and to Descartes in the seventeenth. That argues for the existence of God, or, more properly, of *a* God, on the ground that he, or it, can be contemplated as a being, than which no greater being can be thought. We make that observation because in one way or another the several theistic proofs appear to contain as an element the assumption of the ontological argument. We have left aside for our own stated purposes such arguments as the cosmological proof, or argument from cause, the teleological proof or argument grounded in the assumption of purpose, and arguments from design and from morality.

## The Divine Purchase

Immanuel Kant has presented logical disproofs of the so-called proofs, and while it is not necessary to expand the relevant questions at this point it can be recalled that Kant himself made a theistic argument, embedded in his so-called Copernican revolution in the theory of knowledge. That has had long-running influence on theological doctrine. It emanates, as has been adequately shown already, from Kant's consignment of God to his noumenal realm and the consequential impossibility of knowing God. Kant charitably concluded that God may or may not exist. The assumption of God's existence, however, was for Kant a useful postulate of practical reason, not, as he saw it, a conclusion of pure reason.

But if the question of the *existence* of God were addressed, it could be readily established that final proof exists in what Christian apologetics refers to as "the impossibility of the contrary." By that it is meant that if God did not exist there would be no grounds at all for explanation, reason, or logic. The "contrary" to the statement that God exists would involve either the conclusion, as argued in chapter 2, that whatever happens happens by chance, or that it is the outcome of an inexplicable materialistic determinism. Man himself is then essentially a chance phenomenon or a material entity without real explanation, and the identity of personhood is destroyed, along with responsibility, accountability, and personal ethics.

At an initial stage in chapter 1, we took note of the several ways in which God has made himself known. In the context of our discussion of the human condition it was concluded that man is revelatory of God by reason that he was created as the image of God. In view of its crucial significance we shall return to the point. But it will not be necessary to explore at length the various ways in which, as previously stated, God has made himself known.

The second caveat has to do with the question raised in chapter 12 regarding the necessity and canonicity of Scripture. I have left aside detailed references to the large and important literature that has addressed more expansively the inspiration, authority, and perspicuity of Scripture. As already observed, an extensive and growing literature exists in those areas, and in more recent times theological opinion has called strongly in question the inerrancy of the scriptural text. The question of authorship, meaning by that the primary authorship of the Holy Spirit and the secondary human authorship and the use of material sources, has become clouded.[1] Douglas Kelly's blunt but correct conclusion does not command

---

1. The debate generated by Peter Enns's *Inspiration and Incarnation*, is only one

universal assent: "God reveals Himself... by means of His Word and Spirit personally within the context of the covenant community."[2]

Foremost among the claims of scripturicity is that of the self-attestation of Scripture. That important element of the discussion has been addressed with usually high insight by John Murray and Ned B. Stonehouse.[3] An attempt at this point to present a coverage of the literature of the debate on the Scriptures would inevitably be incomplete, and focus is therefore retained on what are judged to be the two important questions at issue: First, why, in the context of man's relation with God, was, and is, the Scripture necessary; and second, if the Scripture is to be taken as the rule, or the canon, for Christian life, how is canonicity to be accorded to the Old and New Testaments?

To return to the first of our questions, on the matter of presuppositions it is not necessary to be more expansive than has been previously stated, beyond the obviously necessary statement that all reasoning is, and in the nature of the case must be, presuppositional reasoning. Presuppositions, in the general case and by reason that they are presuppositions, do not in and of themselves submit to justification or vindication. They are simply the suppositions on which reason and discourse proceed. But the edifice of reasoning that the presuppositions support can be judged to be significant, valid, interesting, or meaningful, depending on both the directions the reasoning takes as a result of its presuppositional foundations and the conclusions it reaches. In that sense it is open to judgment whether the presuppositional basis of reasoning that is adopted in any particular case is or is not most likely to lead to meaningful and informative results.

In the area of our immediate concern, that of theological-doctrinal argument, two things are to be said. In the first place, the two questions we have raised, that of the possibility of knowing God and the manner in which God has made himself known, come to confluence in the sense that the first rests clearly on the second. That is to say, we presuppose God in all our reasoning precisely *because* God has made himself known in the manner he has. The second thing to be said, therefore, is that because God has made himself known in the Scriptures, the Scriptures themselves are the source of our presuppositions. In our theological-doctrinal reasoning we

---

example of the contemporary disturbed discussions in this area.

2. Kelly, *Systematic Theology*, 13.

3. Murray, "Attestation"; see also Murray, *Calvin on Scripture*; Murray, "The Holy Scriptures"; Stonehouse, *The Infallible Word*.

are not free to choose and elaborate our presuppositions from any source that might be conjured or by an even more ultimate assumption of the competence of autonomous human reason. We cannot simply pluck our presuppositions out of the air or discover them in contemporary intellectual or cultural fashions or assumptions. On the contrary, the source of our presuppositions is precisely the word that God has given in the Scriptures.

The two questions we are now addressing, the knowledge of God and the scripturicity of Scripture, will be seen to be closely related. For if, as we have said, it is possible to know God, it is necessary to ask what is the nature and possible extent of such knowledge. And if, then, as has again already been argued, it is possible to know God because he has made a revelation of himself and thereby has made himself known, why are the Scriptures to be regarded as the authoritative vehicle of that revelation?

In earlier contexts we have observed that the apostle John elaborates an extensive argument to explain that the Christian's highest good in this life is "fellowship with the Father" (1 John 1:3). It is not possible in this life to *see* God with the eyes of flesh, but it is our highest good in this life to *know* God and have fellowship with him. "This is life eternal," our Lord prayed to the Father, "that they might *know* thee" (John 17:3). Moreover, "If we walk in the light, as he is in the light, we have fellowship one with another" (1 John 1:7). The "one with another" at that point in the apostle's letter does not refer to a fellowship that exists between members of the church that Christ has called into being, important though that is in other contexts of the scriptural teaching. The "one with another" in John's immediate context refers to the fellowship that exists between God on the one hand and the Christian person on the other. That accords with the fuller context of John's epistle, in which he explains from repeated perspectives that the Christian's highest good in this life is to have "fellowship with the Father, and with his Son Jesus Christ" (1 John 1:3).

But whom does the apostle present as the possible object of knowledge? Who is God? Or as the Catechism asks, "What is God?" meaning what is God like, or how shall we refer to God as the object of our knowing?[4] We may meditate further on John's continuing argument. "God," he says, "is light, and in him is no darkness at all" (1 John 1:5). But what does it mean to say that God is light? How shall we speak of God? The meaning we would grasp is evasive. Is it possible to define who God is? What shall we say of God, the Creator and sustainer of all that he spoke into existence external

---

4. Westminster Shorter Catechism, Question 4.

## The Knowledge of God

to the Godhead, who exists in three eternal Persons, who established the very temporal process as a mode of our finite existence, whose property we are as a result and to whom we are responsible and accountable?

Our difficulty rests in the fact that we ourselves, as to our being, are the finite analogue of the eternal, infinite God. The very finitude that defines us establishes the fact that it is not possible for us to have comprehensive knowledge of God. The problem of conceiving of the knowledge of God that is available to us derives from the fact that we cannot know God comprehensively. We have said that we can know him truly, that our knowledge of him and of what he knows is true because he has revealed it to us. But that knowledge itself is analogical. The status of the theological explanation has occupied the minds of the theologians historically and is well established. We may put it in the following terms. If it were to be said that what God knows and what man knows or is capable of knowing is precisely the same in content and in words that express the knowledge, then we would be saying that the relation between God's knowledge and our knowledge is "univocal." If, at the opposite extreme, it were claimed that there was no relation at all between God's knowledge and our knowledge, or between God's words and our words, then our claim would be that the relationship was not "univocal" (the same), but "equivocal" (completely different). But we take neither of those opposing positions. We say that the relation between God's knowledge and our knowledge is neither univocal nor equivocal, but that it is analogical. That is, our knowledge is *like* God's knowledge but is not *identical* with God's knowledge. The response has been made that the claim that we have just made implies agnosticism, or, that is, that we cannot really know any absolute truth at all. But such a counterclaim is misguided because on the level of the possibility of knowledge we are speaking about what the true God himself is truthfully communicating to us about the objects of knowledge that in our finite and analogical status of being we are able to assimilate.

Our knowledge, while it is true knowledge as God communicates it to us or makes possible our consciousness of it, is analogical of what God knows in himself for a very practical reason. That is that God in his all-knowing infinity necessarily knows all the interrelations and interactions between all levels and categories of knowledge in a manner that is clearly impossible for us. There is a difference between God and ourselves in the matter of *what* God and we respectively know, and also *how* we know. For us, knowledge, along with the processes of the acquisition of knowledge, is sequential and temporal. For God, who exists in timeless eternity, knowledge is not sequential. God knew all things in one eternal act of knowing. God knows all things because he thought all things in one timeless moment. A response to statements of the difference between God's knowledge and our knowledge may perhaps be made in the following form. It may be claimed, for example, that God knows that David was king of Israel and we know that David was king of Israel, and that, therefore, knowing precisely the same thing, the relation between God's knowledge and our knowledge is univocal. But such a counterclaim misses the mark. For what God knows, which in its comprehensiveness is beyond our grasp, is what it means to the eternal God, in all its implications and relations with everything else that God has ordained, to say that David was king of Israel.

We are unable, therefore, to describe comprehensively who God is or what God knows. We are unable to penetrate to a comprehensive intellectual grasp and understanding of the essence of God. The essence of God is not immediately accessible to us, and what we know of God is what he reveals to us in the divine attributes by which he defines himself. The *essence* of God is revealed in his disclosed *attributes*. The essence of God is referred to in, for example, the *Westminster Confession of Faith*, by saying that "There is but one only living and true God, who is infinite in being and perfection, a most pure spirit, invisible, without body, parts, or passions, immutable, immense, eternal, incomprehensible, almighty, most wise, most holy, most free, most absolute."[5] We see in that confessional statement an attempt to conceive of what is to be said as to the *essence* of God. The Confession then goes on to speak of the *attributes* of God, in terms of which he reveals himself. He is "most loving, gracious, merciful, long-suffering, abundant in goodness and truth.[6]

The distinction between the divine *essence* and divine *attributes* accordingly assumes extreme importance in theological-doctrinal constructions. We have seen that the apostle John concluded in his first epistle that "God is light." We may grasp something of the struggle John had at that point to communicate to his readers what he contemplated as the God about whom he wrote. He wanted to speak of God's infinite excellences, or as the Puritan commentator, Matthew Poole, puts it, of his "absolute simplicity, immutability, knowledge, wisdom, sincerity, righteousness, serenity, benignity, joy, and felicity, and especially of most bright and glorious

5. *Westminster Confession of Faith*, II, 1.
6. Idem, II, 1–2.

holiness and purity."[7] John sums it up by saying that "God is light." But then we must ask the meaning of the statement that God is light.

Perhaps the confessional statement provides us with secure guidance when it says that God is "most holy." But before we ask what is the meaning of holiness in that context, we see that God is, in the ways we have noted, defining himself for our understanding. And the consciousness arises within us that our task, given our capabilities and our prerogatives in the matter of knowing God, is not that of knowing him as he is in himself, but as he is toward us. In that, we have a true and adequate disclosure of who God is, sufficient to guide us, fallen and sinful beings as we are, to the eternal rest in him that he has provided for us in his Son, because he sent his Son into the world to reconcile us to himself.

If we inquire further into the meaning of holiness that the Confession has set before us, we can reflect on the fact that holiness, in one way or another and on a given level, means and implies a separation or a separateness. Is anything to be said, then, of God's separateness? The answer strikes to the very heart of what is revealed to us as the being of God. Let us state that in the following terms.

God is separate from all reality external to the Godhead that he spoke into existence. Beyond that, God exists eternally without cause. It would not be correct to say that God is the cause of his own being and existence. For if that were said it would imply the preexistence of God in order to be his own cause. Rather, we say quite simply that God exists eternally without cause. That, in turn, implies that there did not exist, and there does not exist, any thing, or entity, or law, or possibility external to God in terms of which he defines himself. We are forced to say, then, that God, in his infinity and eternality, existed, in his being and eternal beatitude, before he created space and time into which he proceeded to create all of external reality. In doing the latter, he established not only reality as it exists, but all of the laws of operation of reality, including the laws of human thought, language, and reason. The laws of logic, of right thinking, are not a human invention, but are a divine endowment. Language is not a human invention. It, too, is a divine endowment. Indeed, when we say that man is the image of God in that he is a rational, immortal, spiritual, moral, and speaking person, we are saying that it is the fact that man speaks that differentiates him most notably from the rest of God's sentient creation. Man thinks and speaks

---

7. Poole, *Commentary*, 930.

## The Divine Purchase

because God thinks and speaks. He speaks in order that he can understand the speech of God to him and can speak back to God.

As to the possibility of knowing God, then, man himself is revelatory of God. The God-consciousness that rises inevitably and uninvited in the human soul itself speaks to the being and character of God. Man, conscious in his reflective self-awareness that he is the image of God, knows that he is rational because God is rational. That is why we say that man thinks and speaks because God thinks and speaks. That is well established by the fact that God, in the pre-incarnate appearance of the Second Person of the Godhead, walked and talked with Adam "in the garden in the cool of the day" (Gen 3:8). Because there was, in the naturalness of Adam's unfallen state, that intellectual communication between God and man, it is clear that the mind was then the prince of the faculties of the human soul.

Further, man is immortal in soul because God is immortal. In his first letter to Timothy, Paul states that God "only hath immortality" (1 Tim 6:16). Man, the image of God, has derivative immortality. That immortality of soul will come to its fullest expression in the last great day either in eternal bliss and joy when we see God in the face of Jesus Christ, or in the eternal perdition that sin has warranted. That will come "in the twinkling of an eye" when "the dead shall be raised incorruptible . . . and this mortal shall have put on immortality" (1 Cor 15:52–53). That immortality of soul is saying that man is spiritual because God his maker is spiritual. Again, what is God? the Catechism asks. "God is a spirit, infinite, eternal and unchangeable"[8] That is at its essence the problem with modern man. He has denied his spirituality. That is not meant to say that modern man has no interest in what, in some not-very-well-defined sense, might be reckoned to be spiritual. Satan, who is expert at confusing man by confusing categories of thought, has sidetracked human understanding with his counterfeits in precisely that direction. But man refuses to acknowledge what is true of his human status. In too many instances he thinks he is only a material object, and that a philosophy of materialism adequately defines what he is. But he is primarily and essentially a spiritual being because he came from the hands of the eternal Spirit who is God, and that he lives in what is primarily and essentially a spiritual universe.

As to the revelatory nature of man as the image of God, he is moral because God is moral. That should press on our consciousness in two respects. First, the *sensus deitatis*, the sense of God, which is innate in the

---

8. Westminster Shorter Catechism, Question 4.

human consciousness, speaks to the soul that God is holy and that, as a result, he is eternally righteous. Holiness refers to a state of being. Righteousness has reference to action that is consistent with that state of being. God is righteous in that all his thoughts, deliberations, actions, ordinances, and purposes are consistent with, and derive from, the eternal and immutable holiness that characterizes him and in which he exists. So that in his very constitution man is revelatory of God.

Second, the inescapable fact that man is conscious of his own morality, of an innate judicial sense that distinguishes right behavior from wrong, is itself a confirmation of the existence of God. The human awareness of an inescapable moral sense raises the question of its origin and of what gives sustenance to it and to the certitude (in the normal mind) that morality and moral judgment are necessary for human life. The conclusion presses that the very phenomenon of moral judgment has its source in the Creator God.

But we have it in the statement of the apostle John that God is light. God as light shines into the darkness and dispels the darkness that is man's natural state. We observed in our opening chapters the essential human condition. Our first parents were created in knowledge, righteous, and holiness, and in his natural unfallen state, with his intellectual faculty of mind Adam naturally knew God. We have said that for Adam to *be* was to *know*. With his faculty of affection he naturally loved God. And with his still unsullied volitional faculty or will, he naturally obeyed God in the commandments that God had communicated to him. Our first parent was created in holiness, and in his intrinsic holy state there was the naturalness about his relation with God his maker that we have just observed. Our first parent's holiness was an aspect of his created estate or constitution, not a gift-added-on (a *donum superadditum*) after his creation as some theologies argue. Adam was intrinsically holy, with all the holy relations with God that that implied.

In our first parent's unfallen state, then, the mind was the prince of the faculties of the soul, and with the mind he was in perfectly unsullied, uncluttered communion with God. But as we have already explored at some length, Adam sinned, and his fall brought all mankind into an estate of sin and misery.[9] Now the mind has been "blinded by the god of this world" (2 Cor 4:4), and in all of his faculties of soul man is the slave of Satan and sin. The upshot of the condition in which man now exists is that, while the revelation of God is clear, man has put blinkers on his eyes so that he cannot

---

9. See ibid., 13–19.

see. Paul the apostle has clarified completely that in spite of the fact that the awareness of God is deeply embedded in the soul, and that therefore no man is ignorant of the existence and power of God, nevertheless whenever the awareness of God rises unbidden to the level of consciousness, the natural man suppresses it, pushes it down (Rom 1:18). He proceeds with his claim that God does not exist and hold any authority over him. He effectively denies his creaturehood. Such is the sorry state of man in sin. In his fallen state the mind is no longer the prince of the faculties of the soul. The emotions, the lusts, and the passions have usurped the position of hegemony in the soul.

The implication of that for our present purposes is that in his initial state man was in possession of the true principles of knowledge, truth, and interpretation with which God had endowed him at his creation. But at the fall, man lost the true principles and true categories and criteria of truth and meaning. When, then, the apostle says that God is light, the immediate level on which that has meaning is that the light of God restores to man the principles, categories, and criteria of meaning that were lost in the fall. The Psalmist was conscious of that remarkable and necessary relation between God and man: "With thee is the fountain of life; in thy light shall we see light" (Ps 36:9). The apostle Paul addressed the point. The condition of man in his natural unregenerate state apart from the renewing grace of God is that "The god of this world hath blinded the mind" (2 Cor 4:4). But for his own people, "God, who commanded the light to shine out of darkness [at the first creation], hath shined in our hearts, to give the light of the knowledge of the glory of God in the face of Jesus Christ" (2 Cor 4:6). Light dispels the darkness and provides access to meaning. And that is modern man's greatest need. He desperately needs access to meaning. Apart from the meaning that resides in God and that God imparts, man, as a philosopher has said, is like a blind man in a dark room searching for a black cat that isn't there. Man stands desperately in need of light. That is why the apostle summarizes his meditation with the dictum that God is light.

But what are we to say of the possibility of knowledge of God for the man who has been made the beneficiary of the grace of regeneration? We do not need to retrace at this point what has been said of the source, the meaning, and the effects in the soul of the Holy Spirit's work of regeneration. Suffice it to say that by regeneration a man is introduced to an awareness and knowledge of God that previously was completely foreign to him. Now the mind is enlightened to see what was blank and dark before. Now the heart is warmed to love God who, by his Spirit, has come to draw him to himself in Christ. Now the will is renewed so that the person hastens to Christ with a new freedom and desire. The person may have heard the good news of the gospel a thousand times before, without his having been aware of any sensible meaning in it. But now the gospel comes with a newness that for the first time, with newly opened eyes of the mind, the individual sees and understands what God has been saying all along. For that is the beauty of the gospel. It is the statement of God that explains a man to himself. It is the light of God shining into the soul.

What, then, does the regenerate person know? He knows, in new dimensions though in certainly incomplete but expanding forms, that God is a God of grace and mercy, forgiving sin and conveying to sinners new life that can never die. He knows that when God said in Christ "Come unto me all ye that labour and are heavy laden, and I will give you rest" (Matt 11:28) the verities of heaven had called him to a rest that he had never known. The darkness of mind had cleared now. At last, knowing God who had revealed himself, the person now knows himself in a new way. His sin, he now knows, had outraged the holiness of God and it drives him to repentance and to faith-commitment to Christ. He knows he is secure in Christ, for now and for eternity, for God whom he had scorned all through his years has called him to himself. He knows that the words that God has spoken to him are true. "Thy word is truth" (John 17:17). He now grasps that realization with new relief of soul. He knows that the word of Christ is true when he says "I am the good shepherd . . . I lay down my life for the sheep . . . I give unto them eternal life; and they shall never perish, neither shall any man pluck them out of my hand" (John 10:14, 15, 28).

But more. The individual who now knows God as he has revealed himself knows the company of God by his Holy Spirit as he walks in newness of life to the inheritance that has been prepared for him (Heb 9:15). It is true, profoundly and wonderfully true, that God draws to himself, and opens the floodgates of knowledge to those whom, before the foundation of the world, he chose and gave to his Son to redeem. He says in grace to them: "I have loved thee with an everlasting love; therefore with lovingkindness have I drawn thee" (Jer 31:3). Such a person knows God because he now freely converses with God, he cultivates the presence of God, as John says he now has "fellowship with the Father and with his Son Jesus Christ" (1 John 1:3). In short, the individual knows God because he has at last been reconciled to God.

But that new status contains within itself a knowledge of God in yet further ways. God does not save us to leave us to ourselves. He is our guide, our counsellor and friend who provides for us and leads us home to himself. He ministers his expanding and sanctifying grace to us, and he does that in a way that involves a corresponding knowledge of himself. Let us observe finally how that is so.

We observed that as to the possibility of knowing God a distinction is to be drawn between the *essence* of God, which is not immediately accessible to us, and the *attributes* of God whereby the essence is exhibited in ways and in degrees of God's own choosing. Now it is to be seen that in the Christian life, the life of the one who has come to know God, aspects of the attributes of God will be reflected in him and he will thereby know God increasingly and in expanding aspects. But we must observe, at the same time, that when we speak of the attributes of God we must distinguish between those revealed attributes that are *incommunicable* and those that are *communicable*. By incommunicable attributes of God we refer to those attributes that define, so far as definition is possible, the very being and nature of God as he exists in himself. It is a fact that in our finitude, and in the face of the acknowledged incomprehensibility of God, we can think of the being of God by negation. We think, for example, of the infinity (the negation of finiteness) of God, the eternality (the negation of temporality and time) of God as he exists in eternal timelessness, and the immutability (the negation of change) of God. But while that is so, God's communicable attributes refer to those revealed characteristics of the eternal God that he does communicate to his redeemed people. His communicable attributes include those aspects of his being and existence that in their communication to us make us progressively like him. They include aspects or elements of holiness, love, wisdom, power, justice, goodness, and mercy. For that is the very objective of God's purpose in our sanctification, his making us like himself. "For this is the will of God," the apostle stated to the Thessalonians, "even your sanctification" (1 Thess 4:3).

We have referred to the purpose and the work of God in our sanctification in previous chapters and at this point only two brief references will be made to the sanctifying communication to the Christian believer of the communicable attributes of God. First, in the sovereignty of God those attributes are communicated to the Christian to the extent that, and in the degree that God is preparing him for the place he has been ordained to occupy in the eternal kingdom of glory. At that final time we shall all be alike in that by the ministry to us of the Holy Spirit we shall have been made perfectly holy. We shall be like Christ (1 John 3:2). But there will be differences of reward. We shall not all be alike in the respective places we assume in glory. We who are saved by the grace of God are all vessels designed for his glory. In the last great day we shall all be alike full, but we will not all be alike large.

The final thing to be said in response to the communication to us of the communicable attributes of God takes us back to the central issue that we have had under discussion, namely the nature and possible extent of our knowledge of God. In the Christian individual's walk with God in this life, in his conscious reception of the graces of God in the manner we have now contemplated, he knows God in increasing degree. That is the glory of the Christian life. It is a life in God. It is, as an old Puritan author put it, "the life of God in the soul of man."[10]

Is, then, knowledge of God possible? It is, as was said at the very beginning, because God has revealed himself. We looked in an earlier chapter at the several ways in which his revelation has been made. Among those ways, we have brought to particular emphasis the word that he has given in the inerrant, infallible, and authoritative Scriptures of which he himself, by his Holy Spirit, is the author. It is important for the Christian professor, therefore, to reach a settled conclusion that the Scripture, in all its parts, is the fully inspired word of God to us, and that it provides the only access to true meaning and understanding. It is that of which man in his fallen state is desperately in need. The Scripture provides the only efficient and practical rule of life.

In the following chapter we shall therefore look, again briefly, at the reason why it is to be insisted that the Scriptures as we have them are both necessary and canonical.

---

10. Scougal, *The Life of God in the Soul of Man*.

CHAPTER 12

# The Necessity and Canonicity of Scripture

A HALF CENTURY AGO Martyn Lloyd-Jones began an important study by observing that "If I understand the religious situation at all [the] whole question of authority is one of the most important questions confronting us."[1] He went on to speak of the authority of the Scriptures and concluded that "We are to declare that the entire Bible—the canonical Scriptures of the Old and the New Testaments—is the Word of God. Also, when we speak of the authority of Scripture we mean 'that property by which it demands faith and obedience to all its declarations.'"[2] "The choice for us today," Lloyd-Jones continued, "is really as simple as it was for those first Christians in the early days. We either accept this authority or else we accept the authority of 'modern knowledge,' modern science, human understanding, human ability. It is one or the other."[3]

With the passing of time the situation within the confessing church has only worsened. It would involve a larger essay than is proposed in this space to report adequately on developments and trends in the evangelical church's doctrine of Scripture. Questions of biblical inspiration, authority, and interpretation have given rise to an expanding literature. The contemporary pressure to accommodate evolutionist thought forms has had its deleterious effect. The more modest intention in what follows is to raise several suggestions as to how the questions of the necessity and canonicity of Scripture might be approached, and to underline the necessity for

---

1. Lloyd-Jones, *Authority*, 7.
2. Ibid., 43–44.
3. Ibid., 60.

## The Necessity and Canonicity of Scripture

holding to old and valued traditions in those respects.[4] Our position, in short, is not that the Scriptures *contain* the word of God, but that Scripture in its entirety *is* the word of God. Further, the very words of Scripture in the original autographs are the words of God written by the secondary authors under the infallible inspiration of the primary author, the Holy Spirit.

In the Scriptures God has given us his self-disclosure. Theology, as it derives from that source material, is a product of human activity, knowledge, and intellection. It is in that sense a human science. But the *materials* of theology are in a unique sense of divine origin and they constitute, in essence and origin, the written corpus of divine revelation. The necessity of that revelation, and the forms it has taken, follow from both our finitude and our sin. Our first parents, in their unfallen condition, stood in need of special revelation and in need of a divine introduction to the source of knowledge and the manner of knowing; and the fall into sin occasioned new necessities. Against those realities we shall comment briefly in what follows on several aspects of our subject: first, the necessity of revelation; second, the necessity of Scripture; third, the canonicity of Scripture; fourth, the Canon of the Old Testament; fifth, the Canon of the New Testament; and sixth, the closure of the Canon.

Several preliminary definitions will indicate the nature of the arguments that follow. The presupposition with which discussion in these areas must begin, as it provides the fundamental presupposition of Christian theology and apologetics, is that *God is* and that he has made a revelation to us; and because we see *that* in the Scriptures they convey to us the authority to which we shall refer. For given that the human person is the analogue of God, both as to his being and his knowledge, dependent on God whose image he is for life and understanding, it is only as God has taken the initiative and revealed himself that such knowledge is possible. That implies, in turn, that the necessity of Scripture turns on the necessity of God's self-disclosure and revelation.

An important distinction enters at that point. The necessity of *revelation*, we have said, is due to our *finitude*. The necessity of *Scripture*, the inscripturation of that revelation, is due to our *sin*.

The question of the canonicity of Scripture has been treated extensively in the literature of Old and New Testament introduction. For example, "How

---

4. The following material was expanded in my paper on "The Necessity and Canonicity of Scripture" delivered at the annual meeting of the New England Reformed Congregational Fellowship, May, 2000. Selected paragraphs of what follows were published in Vickers, *Christian Confession*, 64–92.

and when did the Church come to regard these twenty-seven books of the New Testament as an authoritative collection of peculiar books separated from others?"[5] Our primary interest in what follows, however, will not be on the history of the formation of the canon, but with the question, "Upon what grounds has the church accepted these books as canonical and was it warranted in doing so?"[6] In that manner, our interest is directed to the question of why it is that the books of the Scripture as we have them are understood by the church to be the source of the church's authority in its belief and practice. That is, we should dislodge our thought from that of the canon as a mere list of books and look at the fact of, and the reasons for, the *authority* that those books have been seen by the mind of the church to possess.[7]

The perspective we have established implies that the necessity and the authority of the Scriptures are to be seen as interdependent. The Scriptures as God's revelation that he has accommodated to our sinful condition are authoritative because they are necessary. And by reciprocal argument, the Scriptures are necessary because it was necessary that God should make a gracious and authoritative revelation to us if we were to have any true knowledge of him, any true knowledge of created reality external to the Godhead that he spoke into existence, and knowledge of what he requires of us. The Scriptures are necessary because it is only through the lens provided by the revelation of the Scriptures that nature can be read correctly.

Without the Scriptures the truth of natural revelation is distorted. They provide the extramundane "Archimedean point," or the only ground on which we can stand to explain ourselves, our own personal significance, and the universe of reality in which we exist. The reference to the "Archimedean point" has in view the philosophers who speak of the necessity of a point outside the world, or an extra-mundane point, on which to stand in order to understand the world. Among the many accomplishments of the Greek philosopher-mathematician, Archimedes, was his discovery of the principle of the lever. On that principle he said, "Give me a place on which to stand and I will move the world." It was obvious that such a point could not be *within* the world if the world was to be moved. It must be an extra-mundane

---

5. Ridderbos, "The Canon of the New Testament," in Henry, *Revelation*, 189–201. See also Harrison, *Introduction*, 91–128; Muller, *Post-Reformation Reformed Dogmatics*, 371–441; Young, "The canon of the Old Testament," in Henry, op. cit., 153–68.

6. Ridderbos, op. cit., 189.

7. In adopting this angle of vision on the question of canonicity and authority I do not intend to diminish the importance and the necessity of scholarly studies in the history of the canon. See, for example, Metzger, *Canon*, and Wenham, *Christ and the Bible*.

point. Transferring the notion to the question of understanding the world, or in our present case understanding the scope of what God has revealed about the world and his purposes in relation to it, we are in need again of an extra-mundane point on which to stand. Our Lord articulated such a point when he said in his high priestly prayer: "I have manifested thy name unto the men which thou gavest me . . . *and they have kept thy word*" (John 17:6, italics added). That states precisely the ground on which we stand. It is the unbreakable Word of God (John 10:35) that provides our starting point and our guide and enlightens our journey in all its stages.[8]

The angle of vision that sees the Scriptures as canonically normative is determined by the fact that in the New Testament the word "*kanon*" is used to carry the connotation of a "rule" or a "standard." At Philippians 3:16, for example, we have, "let us walk by the same rule" (κανόνι, *kanoni* in the Textus Receptus, the Greek text from which the KJV was translated), though the word "rule" is omitted from the modern Greek text and the ESV translation. At Galatians 6:16, both the Textus Receptus and the modern text contain the word "rule" (*kanoni*) which appears in translation as "walk according to this rule." Both the text sources I have mentioned employ derivatives of the same Greek word to mean a rule or a standard in 2 Corinthians 10:13, 15. The lexicographers lead us to believe that "In the second century in the Christian church '*kanon*' came to stand for revealed truth, *rule of faith*."[9]

## The necessity of revelation

The essential need of the human self, who stands in his world as the analogue of God, is knowledge, or true knowledge of God and the world. That knowledge is attainable and assimilable only because God has revealed himself. Our immediate object is to take account of, first, the necessity and the *fact* of God's revelation, before we address the question of the necessity

---

8. The Reformed theological apologetic of Cornelius Van Til underlines this necessity when he states that "Christ's work is of cosmic significance. . . . There is through him and through his Word an authoritative interpretation given to mankind of the whole of the cosmic scene. Every fact in the universe must be Christologically interpreted." Van Til, *Christian Theory of Knowledge*, 30–31. Reymond has spoken of the necessity of an extra-mundane starting point in addressing the doctrine of Scripture as "A Word from Another World" in his *New Systematic Theology*, xxxvii. See also idem 56, n. 2, and the same author's *Justification of Knowledge*, 32.

9. Bauer et al., *Greek-English Lexicon*, 403.

of the *form* in which that revelation has been made. In a more extensive review it would be profitable to reflect on those various forms: first, in the created reality in which we exist; second, in man's own constitution by reason that he was established as the image, or the analogue, of God, in the light of which God has kept open the channels of communication to man; third, in the history of God's providential government of the world, and particularly in his ordering of the redemptive history of his people; fourth, in the Scriptures; and finally in his Son (Heb 1:1–2).

In his unfallen state Adam naturally knew God, and he knew with unsullied clarity what God revealed to him as the meaning of reality. For Adam, *to be* was *to know*. He possessed an uncluttered receptivity of God's revelation to him. The puzzle of man's condition now in his fallen state is essentially the problem of knowledge, an epistemological question. It is the question of whether true knowledge is attainable, of what is the origin and source of true knowledge, the legitimate processes of its discovery, the criteria of validity in knowledge, and the reasons why what is known can be claimed to be true. Because at Adam's fall we surrendered the possibility of what I have referred to as true knowledge, the understanding of that puzzling condition conducts us to the fact and the necessity of Scripture.

But in relation to the question of knowledge and meaning, our starting point must of necessity be, as we have stated, the presupposition of God as he exists and has revealed himself. We may say quite properly that because it is we ourselves who are entering the knowledge process, we start with ourselves as what we may call our psychological starting point. We start with ourselves in that psychological sense because we are conscious of our own personhood, and there is therefore nowhere else to start. But if we are our own *psychological* starting point, it is equally clear that the presupposition of God is our *epistemological* starting point.[10]

But the problem facing us is that, in his fallen condition, man has no true access to knowledge. By virtue of the *sensus deitatis*, the sense of God, embedded in the soul, he has an ineradicable cognition of the existence of God, and even of the power of God (Rom 1:20). But he cannot know God as he has revealed himself and he cannot know God savingly (John 17:3) because his mind is blinded by the god of this world (2 Cor 4:4). In his condition in sin, man knows God as Creator, but not as Redeemer.

---

10. This distinction is similar to that between an *immediate* or *temporal* or *proximate* starting point and an *ultimate* starting point raised by Van Til in his *Survey of Christian Epistemology*, 120, 130. See also Notaro who distinguishes between the *logical* and the *epistemological* starting points in *Van Til & The Use of Evidence*, 82.

While that is so, he cannot know anything of created reality truly because he cannot know, and he sinfully suppresses every wakening awareness of the possibility of knowing (Rom 1:18) that all the facts of reality are what they are because they are God's facts. He cannot know that the facts exist in the constellations and coherences they exhibit because of the place they occupy in the plan of God.

It follows that only those know truly who know God truly. Of course it is true that the non-Christian, the unregenerate person, can make true statements about the relations of forces that exist in created reality. Legitimacy attaches clearly to many of the achievements of unregenerate science and the advances that have been made in the betterment of human society as a result. But it is a short argument to establish that it is only because of the operation of God's common grace that unregenerate individuals can and do make such statements of truth. Such statements are possible only because the universe is, in fact, structured by God-created laws and is not the universe of randomness and chance that apostate thought imagines it to be. Apostate man must necessarily stand on God's ground in order to make the claim that God does not exist. That is the irony of all forms of non-Christian philosophy and non-Christian systems of thought.

## The necessity of Scripture

When we speak of the Scriptures we are speaking of a particular form of God's revelation. While the necessity of revelation as such is grounded, on our side, in our finitude, the necessity of Scripture is grounded in our sin. Two implications follow immediately from that fact. First, apart from God's initiative in making his inscripturated revelation available to us, we should have remained without any true knowledge of him and of what he requires of us. The explanation of our sinfulness is patent on the very surface of Scripture; and we claim the necessity of Scripture on the ground that the exigency of sin means that general or natural revelation is insufficient to provide that knowledge of God that is necessary to salvation. Secondly, therefore, the revelation that God has made in the Scriptures is to be seen as primarily a redemptive revelation. We have there the explanation of the perilous state to which, in Adam, we had fallen, and the provision that was made for our redemption in terms of the covenant that God the Father established with the Son and the Holy Spirit before the foundation of the world. The necessity of the Scriptures inheres, then, in the requirements inherent in the eternally established decree of redemption. That means that the revelation in the Scriptures is a covenantal revelation.

From God's side it was not, of course, necessary that a plan of redemption should be set forth for the salvation of any of fallen humanity. God's justice and holiness would have remained inviolate if Adam and all his fallen posterity had been left to the eternal perdition their sin warranted. But notwithstanding its non-necessity from God's side, a redemption was in fact decreed, and it was absolutely necessary, as a result, that the eternal Son of God should come into the world as our redeemer. As that eternal decree of grace had been formulated in the counsels of the Godhead, it was similarly necessary that a means of disclosure and education should be established, first as to our need of redemption, and secondly as to the means of redemption that God provided.

It would be a mistake, of course, to say that there had been no redemptive revelation before the purpose of God was inscripturated. The content and purpose of pre-scriptural revelation are clear, to the extent that they have been subsequently recorded in the pages of Scripture itself. It would be a mistake also to conclude that the Scriptures as we have them contain the full revelation that God has made. The situation is clearly as John has observed on it at the conclusion of his gospel. If all that God has done in Christ were recorded, the world could not contain all the books that would need to be written (John 21:25). And we have references in 2 Chronicles 9:29 to prophetic books that have not survived. Moreover, by virtue of the deficiencies and defects of our cognitive capacities that were introduced by our state of sin, we have, on this side of eternity, only a partial and incomplete understanding of the partial revelation that God has preserved to us in the Scriptures.

But while that is so, given the necessity that we should be brought to a salvific understanding both of our own position and the provision for redemption that God has made, the Scriptures have addressed that necessity in several ways. First, we have in clear propositional terms as well as in poetical imagery, the revelation of God's merciful intention and means of redemption. The Scriptures constitute a covenantal, redemptive-historical revelation.[11] That revelation is made "in intelligible statements that convey publicly identifiable meaning."[12] It is an objective, cognitively assimilable, historical revelation.

---

11. See Gaffin, *Perspectives on Pentecost*, 97.
12. Henry, *God, Revelation and Authority*, 45.

Secondly, we have, in clearly understandable, if anthropomorphic terms, a disclosure, not only of God's will and purpose, but of his immanent relation to created reality and its history. His revelation has been made in terms that are cognizable and amenable to our understanding with the creaturely finite comprehension that we possess.

Thirdly, we have in the Scriptures redemptive history, the history of God's people recorded in such a way as to make clear that it was conducted in the way it was for the purpose of bringing into the world the promised Messiah, the Son of God, the seed of the woman who would crush the head of the serpent. The Scriptures constitute both redemptive revelation and redemptive history.

The necessity of the Scriptures inheres finally in the necessity that God should make available to us a permanent record of his redemptive revelation, intentions, and actions. The integrity of the revelation was not entrusted to oral transmission and to the possibilities of its being tarnished by the imperfections of sinful men. Holy men spoke as they were moved by the Holy Spirit (2 Pet 1:21), who is thus the Author of the Scriptures, and their record is true, reliable, inerrant, authoritative, and absolutely trustworthy. The inspired record has been preserved by the overruling providence of God, and its necessity and authority continue until we see our redeemer face to face, until, as Peter says, "the day dawns" (2 Pet 1:19–21).

## The canonicity of Scripture

The question of canonicity has to do with the grounds on which, and the reasons why the church has historically accepted the Scriptures as the authoritative Word of God. Claims to the contrary have, of course, been made and continue to be made in the present day. In the heady atmosphere of contemporary postmodernism, the Bible has been subjected to the same processes of deconstruction that have been brought to bear on the reading of literature in general. The claim is made that the Bible *becomes* the Word of God to an individual reader as a radical subjectivism displaces the objectively given words of God. Noel Weeks has referred to the situation as a "psychological relativism" or a "hermeneutical circle," where the individual sees confirmed in the Bible the interpretative ideas he brings to it. "He reads out of the Bible what he reads into it."[13]

---

13. Weeks, *Sufficiency of Scripture*, 81.

How, then, is, or was, the canonical authority of the Word of God established? Our answer, in short, is that the canonicity of the Scriptures was recognized from the beginning, not because it was the subject of a deliverance by any council of the church (though I shall comment briefly on certain conciliar commendations of canonicity), but by virtue of the internal self-attestation of the Scriptures themselves. The church did not set about to decide inductively what books were worthy of canonization, though we know that different churchmen at different times registered difficulty in recognizing the internal testimony of certain books. Luther's earlier and well-known problem with the book of James, "an epistle of straw" he at first called it, is a case in point. But the church from the earliest times recognized the books as written to be canonical by reason of the source from which, and the manner in which, they were received. The Holy Spirit who gave the Word confirmed in the consciousness of the church that the Word as given was divinely inspired and self-attesting, and that it was therefore to be received as authoritatively canonical. Consider, in that light, the canonicity of the Old and New Testaments.

## The canon of the Old Testament

A summary discussion of the canonicity of the Old Testament can proceed under three heads: first, the statements of the speakers and writers to whom the revelation of God was given; second, the immediacy of the recognition by the Old Testament church of the canonical claims of the revelation; and third, the confirmation by the New Testament of the Old Testament's canonicity, including the imprimatur placed upon it by both our Lord himself and the apostles.

Indications abound in the Old Testament that the writers understood themselves to be conveying the authoritative Word of God. God declared to Moses, "I will be with thy mouth, and teach thee what thou shalt say" (Ex 4:12). And God continued to speak to Moses "face to face," or "mouth to mouth," and "plainly" (Num 12:8). The Old Testament contains numerous instances of the prophetic formula, "Thus saith the LORD," and declarations by the prophets that they were conveying the content of a vision received at the hand of God. The statements, "The vision of Isaiah" (Isa 1:1), "In the year king Uzziah died I saw also the Lord" (Isa 6:1), "The words of Jeremiah . . . to whom the word of the LORD came" (Jer 1:1–2), "Then said the LORD unto me, Though Moses and Samuel stood before me . . ." (Jer

15:1), are only examples of the method of the prophets' reception of divine communication. The same is reported consistently by the Minor Prophets also.

It is clear that God intended that what was thus delivered by and through the prophets should be permanently recorded for the guidance and benefit of the church. Jeremiah, for example, was instructed by God to "take a roll of a book and write therein all the words that I have spoken unto thee" (Jer 36:2). And the sequel reveals that when Jeremiah's script was read to king Jehoiakim and thrown by him into the fire, Jeremiah was enabled again to take "another roll, and [he] gave it to Baruch the scribe . . . who wrote therein . . . all the words of the book which Jehoiakim king of Judah had burned . . . and there were added besides unto them many like words" (Jer 36:32). The prophet Habakkuk was told, "Write the vision, and make it plain upon tables, that he may run that readeth it" (Hab 2:2).

Two implications follow from what has just been said. First, God, by the ministry of his Holy Spirit, confirms his own Word to his regenerate people. Our Lord stated the same point when he said that "My sheep hear my voice" (John 10:27). It is one of the blessings of regeneration that the Spirit of God opens the eyes of the understanding to see the self-attestation of the Scriptures as they have been given. Then it follows that it is God, and not men, who determines whether a book is to belong to the church's canon.[14]

There is evidence that the Old Testament books were recognized as canonical by God's people as soon as they were received. For the book of the law was placed, with the Ark of the Covenant, in the most holy place of the Tabernacle; the priests were to read the law to the people; and it is clearly said that the Exile occurred because of the people's disregard of the law and their transgressions of it. That means that the Word of God as given was accepted as such, and that its acceptance did not depend on the pronouncement of any Council or Synod convened for that purpose.

Further, the canonicity of the Old Testament is confirmed by the attestation of the apostles and our Lord himself. Edward J. Young observes that "Christ recognized as canonical the same books as those which comprise the Old Testament as we have it today."[15] Jesus repeatedly referred to the Law and the Prophets and cited them to settle a matter of dispute. In his Sermon on the Mount he said that he came not "to destroy the law, or the

---

14. See Young, "The Canon of the Old Testament," 155–57.
15. Young, "Authority of the Old Testament," in Stonehouse and Woolley, *The Infallible Word*, 57.

prophets . . . but to fulfill" (Matt 5:17). The Old Testament Scriptures, Christ said to the Jews, "cannot be broken," when he referred on one occasion to what had been "written in your law" (John 10:34–35). "These are the words which I spake unto you, while I was yet with you." Christ said "That all things must be fulfilled, which were written in the law of Moses, and in the prophets, and in the psalms, concerning me" (Luke 24:44). Christ is the church's final authority. He is himself the church's ultimate "canon."

## The canon of the New Testament

The canonicity of the New Testament parallels what has been said regarding the canon of the Scriptures in their entirety. Ned B. Stonehouse concluded that "This authority [of the New Testament] is conceived of, not as superimposed upon the writings at a time when their true character had become obscured or hidden, but as an authority which the books possessed from the very moment of their origin."[16] Robert Reymond has concurred: "The post-apostolic church did not 'canonize' the New Testament Scriptures but only declared that it had received them as authoritative and thus normative from the beginning as an inspired body of literature."[17, 18]

Christ set his seal on the New Testament writings. On the night on which he was betrayed he gave his disciples the promise that "the Comforter, which is the Holy Ghost, whom the Father will send in my name, he shall teach you all things, and bring all things to your remembrance, whatsoever I have said unto you" (John 14:26). And "the Comforter . . . whom I will send unto you . . . even the Spirit of truth . . . he shall testify of me" (John 15:26). "When he, the Spirit of truth is come he will guide you into all truth" (John 16:13). Then Christ confirmed the testimony of the apostles by giving to them the "signs of an apostle" (2 Cor 12:12) to authenticate their ministry and their record of his teaching. The writings of Paul present a special case. Peter makes the familiar statement that places the letters of Paul on a level of parity with "other scriptures," meaning by

16. Stonehouse, "Authority of the New Testament," in Stonehouse and Woolley, *The Infallible Word*, 89.

17. Reymond, *Systematic Theology*, 11.

18. Some churchmen did have difficulty in recognizing the internal testimony of certain books, witness our reference above to Luther on the book of James. The earliest list of the twenty-seven books of the New Testament occurs in a letter of Athanasius in the year 367AD, and the first Council of the church to affirm these twenty-seven books was the Third Council of Carthage in 397AD. See Reymond, op. cit., idem.

that term the Scriptures of the Old Testament (2 Pet 3:16). In Paul's letter to the Thessalonians he said "Ye received the word of God which ye heard of us . . . not as the word of men, but as it is in truth, the word of God" (1 Thess 2:13).

Additionally, internal testimonies of the New Testament confirm that, as in the case of the Old Testament, the church recognized immediately its canonicity, on the grounds that it displays God's faithfulness in fulfilling his covenantal promises. It displays Christ as the antitype of all the Old Testament messianic types, and the recognition of that provides the awareness of its canonicity.

Leaving aside the large and important literature on the history of the canon that is readily available, it is clear that the Spirit of God providentially led his church to recognize that the books we now have in the canon authenticated and established themselves as the inspired, infallible, sufficient, and authoritative Word of God.

## The closure of the canon

We hold that the Scriptural canon as we have it in the sixty-six books of the Bible has been closed. Our confessional standards rightly state that God has committed his revelation "to writing; which makes the Holy Scripture to be most necessary, those former ways of God's revealing his will unto his people, being now ceased."[19]

The closure of the thirty-nine books of the Old Testament is beyond argument. They were held as canonical by the Jews at the time of our Lord, by Christ himself, and by the apostles and the early church.[20] The question of the closure of the canon in the New Testament literature has opened issues that continue to trouble the church. The sufficiency and authority of the New Testament as we have it in twenty-seven books has come under attack in regard to its revelation of the Person and work of Jesus Christ, its directives as to the form of government and administration of the church, and its declarations regarding the manner in which God has stated he desires to be worshiped.

A final and at this time a very troubling question remains, namely that of the cessation of the charismata. Leaving aside important details of the relevant arguments, two final comments will suffice. First, the extraordinary

---

19. *Westminster Confession of Faith*, I:1.
20. See our Lord's assertion in Luke 24:44.

and temporary gifts of the Spirit that are frequently referred to as the charismata, among them notably the gifts of prophecy, healing, and the so-called speaking in tongues, to take instances that currently occupy the mind of the church, are to be understood to have been given to the apostles for the purpose of authenticating their apostolicity. Second, the exercise of those gifts was essentially revelatory.[21] That revelatory significance and the function of the gifts is relevant to what has to be said regarding the closure of the canon.[22]

If we argue for the continuation of the charismata, we are arguing for the continuation of revelation and we claim thereby that revelation is not yet complete. By taking such a position we would be in direct contradiction of the Scripture that tells us that *"in these last days"* God has spoken to us by his Son (Heb 1:2). And we would, of course, contradict the very words with which the canon as God has given it to us has closed (Rev 22:19). God now has nothing to say to man that he has not already said. God has said his last word to man.

---

21. See Gaffin, Jr., *Perspectives on Pentecost*, 89–116. Note Gaffin's discussion of "The inspired and revelatory character of tongues" at 78–81. For wide-ranging discussions see also Coppes, *Whatever Happened to Biblical Tongues*; Chantry, *Signs of the Apostles*. For an alternative view see Carson, *Showing the Spirit*. Robertson, *The Final Word*, responds to Gruden who argues for a modified continuity of the New Testament gift of prophecy and revelation in his *The Gift of Prophecy*. See also Reymond, *New Systematic Theology*, 57 n. 5.

22. See 1 Corinthians 13:2, 1 Corinthians 14:2, Ephesians 3:3–5 for the revelatory significance of both "prophecy" and "tongues" in the light of their relation to "mysteries" and the revelatory connotation of "mystery" in the Pauline vocabulary and literature.

# Bibliography

à Brakel, Wilhelmus. *The Christian's Reasonable Service.* 4 vols. Translated by Bartel Elshout. Edited by Joel R. Beeke. Grand Rapids: Reformation Heritage Books, 1993.
Abrams, M. H., et al, eds. *The Norton Anthology of English Literature.* New York: Norton, 1962.
Bauer, Walter, et al. *A Greek-English Lexicon of the New Testament and Other Early Christian Literature.* Chicago: University of Chicago Press, 1957.
Beeke, Joel R. "The Apostle John and the Puritans on the Father's Adopting, Transforming Love." In *The Beauty and Glory of the Father*, edited by Joel R. Beeke, 79–105. Grand Rapids: Reformation Heritage Books, 2013.
———. *Heirs with Christ: The Puritans on Adoption.* Grand Rapids: Reformation Heritage Books, 2008.
———. "The Puritans on Adoption." In *A Puritan Theology: Doctrine for Life.* Edited by Joel R. Beeke and Mark Jones, 537–54. Grand Rapids: Reformation Heritage Books, 2012.
———, and Mark Jones. *A Puritan Theology: Doctrine for Life.* Grand Rapids: Reformation Heritage Books, 2012.
———, et al. eds. *The Reformation Heritage KJV Study Bible.* Grand Rapids: Reformation Heritage Books, 2014.
Berkhof, L. *Systematic Theology.* Grand Rapids: Eerdmans, 1939.
Berry, George Ricker. *The Interlinear Translation of the Greek New Testament.* Chicago: Handy Book Co., 1897. Republished Grand Rapids: Zondervan, 1958.
Brown, John. *An Exposition of the Epistle of Paul to the Galatians.* Minneapolis: Klock & Klock, 1981.
Brown, Robert K., and Philip W. Comfort, *The New Greek-English Interlinear New Testament.* Wheaton, Ill: Tyndale House, 1990.
Buchanan, James. *The Doctrine of Justification.* Edinburgh: Banner of Truth, 1984.
Calvin, John. *Institutes of the Christian Religion.* 2 vols. Translated by Ford Lewis Battles. Edited by John T. McNeill. Philadelphia: Westminster, 1960.
Candlish, Robert S. *A Commentary on 1 John. Two volumes in one.* Edinburgh: Banner of Truth, 1973.
Carson, D. A. *Showing the Spirit: A Theological Exposition of 1 Corinthians 12–14.* Grand Rapids: Baker, 1987.
Chantry, W. J. *Signs of the Apostles.* Edinburgh: Banner of Truth, 1976.

## Bibliography

Coleridge, Samuel Taylor. *The Complete Poetical Works of Samuel Taylor Coleridge.* Edited by Ernest Hartley Coleridge. Oxford: Clarendon, 1912.
*Congregational Praise.* London: Independent Press for the Congregational Union of England and Wales, 1951.
Coppes, Leonard J. *Whatever Happened to Biblical Tongues.* Phillipsburg, NJ: Pilgrim, 1977.
Dabney, Robert L. *Discussions: Evangelical and Theological, Volume 1.* Edinburgh: Banner of Truth, 1967.
Edwards, Jonathan. *An Inquiry into the Freedom of the Will.* Morgan, PA: Soli Deo Gloria, 1996.
Enns, Peter. *Inspiration and Incarnation: Evangelicals and the Problem of the Old Testament.* Grand Rapids: Baker, 2005.
Eveson, Philip, H. *The Great Exchange: Justification by faith alone – in the light of recent thought.* Leominster, UK: Day One Publications, 1996.
Frame, John. *Systematic Theology: An Introduction to Christian Belief.* Phillipsburg, NJ: P&R, 2013.
Gaffin, Richard B. Jr. *Perspectives on Pentecost.* Phillipsburg, NJ: P&R, 1979.
Gruden, Wayne A. *The Gift of Prophecy in 1 Corinthians.* Lanham: University Press of America, 1982.
Harrison, Everett F. *Introduction to the New Testament.* Grand Rapids: Eerdmans, 1964.
Hendriksen, William. *New Testament Commentary: Exposition of the Gospel According to John.* 2 vols. Grand Rapids: Baker, 1954.
Henry, Carl F. H. *God, Revelation and Authority, Volume 1: God who speaks and shows.* Waco, TX: Word Books, 1976.
———. *Revelation and the Bible.* Grand Rapids: Baker, 1958.
Hodge, A. A. *Outlines of Theology.* Edinburgh: Banner of Truth, 1972.
Kant, Immanuel. *Critique of Practical Reason.* Translated by Thomas Kingsmill Abbott. Originally published 1788. New York: Barnes & Noble, 2004.
———. *Critique of Pure Reason.* Translated by J. M. D. Meiklejohn. Originally published in 1781. New York: Barnes & Noble, 2004.
Kelly, Douglas. "Adoption: An Underdeveloped Heritage of the Westminster Standards." In *Reformed Theological Review,* 52 (1993), 110–20.
———. *Systematic Theology. Volume One: Grounded in Holy Scripture and understood in the light of the Church.* Fearn, Scotland: Christian Focus, 2008.
Knowling, R. J. *The Acts.* In *The Expositor's Greek New Testament,* 5 vols., edited by W. Robertson Nicoll, 2:3–554. Grand Rapids: Eerdmans, 1979.
Kuyper, Abraham. *The Work of the Holy Spirit.* Grand Rapids: Eerdmans, 1956.
Lloyd-Jones, D. Martyn. *Authority.* Chicago: Inter-Varsity, 1958.
Marshall, Alfred. *The Greek-English New Testament.* London: Samuel Bagster, 1958.
Metzger, Bruce. *The Canon of the New Testament: Its Origin, Development, and Significance.* Oxford: Clarendon, 1987.
Morris, Leon. *The Apostolic Preaching of the Cross.* Grand Rapids: Eerdmans, 1955.
Muller, Richard A. *Post-Reformation Reformed Dogmatics, Volume 2, Holy Scripture: The Cognitive Foundation of Theology.* Grand Rapids; Baker 1993.
Murray, John. "The Adamic Administration." In John Murray. *Collected Writings of John Murray,* 2:47–59. Edinburgh: Banner of Truth, 1977.
———. "The Attestation of Scripture." In *The Infallible Word,* edited by N. B. Stonehouse and Paul Woolley, 1–52. Grand Rapids: Eerdmans, 1946.

# Bibliography

———. *Calvin on Scripture and Divine Sovereignty*. Grand Rapids: Baker, 1960.

———. *The Collected Writings of John Murray*. 4 vols. Edinburgh: Banner of Truth, various dates.

———. *The Covenant of Grace*. London: Tyndale, 1954.

———. "Covenant Theology." In John Murray. *Collected Writings of John Murray*, 4:216-40. Edinburgh: Banner of Truth, 1982.

———. "Definitive sanctification." In John Murray. *Collected Writings of John Murray*, 2:277-93. Edinburgh: Banner of Truth, 1977.

———. *The Epistle to the Romans, Volume 1 - Chapters 1 to 8*. Grand Rapids: Eerdmans, 1959.

———. "The Holy Scriptures." In *Collected Writings of John Murray*, 1:1-26. Edinburgh: Banner of Truth, 1976.

———. "Progressive sanctification." In John Murray. *Collected Writings of John Murray*, 2:294-304. Edinburgh: Banner of Truth, 1977.

———. *Redemption - Accomplished and Applied*. Grand Rapids: Eerdmans, 1955.

Newman, John Henry. "Praise to the Holiest in the height." In *Congregational Praise*, 71. London: Independent Press for the Congregational Union of England and Wales, 1951.

Nicoll, W. Robertson. *The Expositor's Greek Testament*. 5 vols. Grand Rapids: Eerdmans, 1979.

Notaro, Thom. *Van Til & The Use of Evidence*. Phillipsburg, NJ: P&R, 1980.

Owen, John. *An Exposition of the Epistle to the Hebrews*. 9 vols. Grand Rapids: Baker, 1980.

———. *Pneumatologia: A Discourse Concerning the Holy Spirit*. In *The Works of John Owen*, 3:1-651. London: Banner of Truth, 1965.

———. *The Works of John Owen*. 16 vols. London: Banner of Truth, 1965.

Poole, Matthew. *A Commentary on the Holy Bible, Volume III: Matthew - Revelation* Edinburgh: Banner of Truth, 1963.

Pope, Alexander. *An Essay on Man*. In *The Norton Anthology of English Literature*, edited by M. H. Abrams et al., 762-70. New York: Norton, 1962.

Reymond, Robert L. *The Justification of Knowledge*. Phillipsburg, NJ: P&R, 1976.

———. *A New Systematic Theology of the Christian Faith*. Nashville: Nelson, 1998.

Ridderbos, Herman. "The Canon of the New Testament." In *Revelation and the Bible*, edited by Carl F. H. Henry, 187-201. Grand Rapids: Baker, 1958.

Robertson, O. Palmer. *The Final Word: A Biblical Response to the Case for Tongues and Prophecy Today*. Edinburgh: Banner of Truth, 1993.

Rogers, A. K. *A Student's History of Philosophy*. New York: Macmillan, 1932.

*Savoy Declaration of Faith*. Various editions.

Scougal, Henry. *The Life of God in the Soul of Man*. Harrisonburg, VA: Sprinkle, 1986.

*Second London (Baptist) Confession*. Various editions.

Sproul, R. C. *Everyone's a Theologian: An Introduction to Systematic Theology*. Sanford, FL: Reformation Trust, 2014.

Stonehouse, N. B. *The Authority of the New Testament*. In *The Infallible Word*. Edited by N. B. Stonehouse and Paul Wolley, 88-136. Grand Rapids: Eerdmans, 1946.

———, and Paul Woolley. *The Infallible Word: A Symposium by the faculty of Westminster Theological* Seminary. Grand Rapids: Eerdmans, 1946.

Trumper, Tim J. R. *When History Teaches Us Nothing: The Recent Reformed Sonship Debate in Context*. Eugene, OR: Wipf & Stock, 2008.

# Bibliography

Turretin, Francis. *Institutes of Elenctic Theology.* 3 vols. Translated by George Musgrave Giger. Edited by James T. Dennison. Phillipsburg, NJ: P&R, 1994.

Van der Pool, Charles. *The Apostolic Bible Polyglot.* Newport, OR: Apostolic Press, 1996.

Van Til, Cornelius. *A Christian Theory of Knowledge.* Philadelphia: Presbyterian and Reformed, 1969.

———. *Survey of Christian Epistemology.* Philadelphia: Den Dulk Foundation, 1969.

Vickers, Douglas. *Christian Confession and the Crackling Thorn: The Imperatives of Faith in an Age of Unbelief.* Grand Rapids: Reformation Heritage Books, 2004.

———. *The Cross: Its Meaning and Message in a Postmodern World.* Eugene, OR: Wipf & Stock, 2010.

———. *Divine Redemption and the Refuge of Faith.* Grand Rapids: Reformation Heritage Books, 2005.

———. *The Texture of Truth.* Grand Rapids: Reformation Heritage Books, 2007.

Weeks, Noel. *The Sufficiency of Scripture.* Edinburgh: Banner of Truth, 1988.

Wenham, John W. *Christ and the Bible.* Guildford, UK: Eagle, 1993.

Wesley, Charles. "Hark! The herald angels sing." In *Congregational Praise*, 84. London: Independent Press for the Congregational Union of England and Wales, 1951.

*Westminster Confession of Faith.* Various editions.

Westminster Shorter Catechism. Various editions.

Witsius, Herman. *The Economy of the Covenants between God and Man.* 2 vols. Phillipsburg, NJ: P&R, 1990.

Young, Edward J. "The Authority of the Old Testament." In N. B. Stonehouse and Paul Woolley, *The Infallible Word*, 53–87. Grand Rapids: Eerdmans, 1946.

———. *The Book of Isaiah.* 3 vols. Grand Rapids: Eerdmans, 1972.

———. "The Canon of the Old Testament." In *Revelation and the Bible*, edited by Carl F. H. Henry, 153–68. Grand Rapids: Baker, 1958.

www.ingramcontent.com/pod-product-compliance
Lightning Source LLC
Chambersburg PA
CBHW071509150426
43191CB00009B/1459